SUZANNE FALKINER is a Sydney writer. The author of twelve previous books of fiction and non-fiction, her most recent titles include the biographies *Joan in India*, 2008, and *The Imago: E. L. Grant Watson & Australia*, 2011. She has been shortlisted in the Vogel Award, the Kibble Award, the Queensland Premier's Literary Award, and the NSW History Awards.
www.suzannefalkiner.com

By the same author

Fiction
Rain In The Distance (1986)
After The Great Novelist And Other Stories (1989)

Non-fiction and biography
Eugenia: A Man (1988)
The Writer's Landscape: Wilderness & Settlement (1992)
Ethel: A Love Story (1996)
Lizard Island: The Journey Of Mary Watson (2001)
with artist Alan Oldfield
Joan In India (2008)
The Imago: E. L. Grant Watson & Australia (2011)

Suzanne FALKINER

Mrs Mort's Madness

XOUM PUBLISHING

Sydney

First published by Xoum in 2014
Xoum Publishing
PO Box Q324, QVB Post Office,
NSW 1230, Australia
www.xoum.com.au

ISBN 978-1-922057-90-7 (digital)
ISBN 978-1-922057-91-4 (print)

All rights reserved. Without limiting the rights under copyright below, no part of this publication shall be reproduced, stored in or introduced into a retrieval system, or transmitted in any form or by any means (electronic, mechanical, photocopying, recording or otherwise), without the prior permission of both the copyright holder and the publisher.

The moral right of the author has been asserted.

Text copyright © Suzanne Falkiner 2014
Cover and internal design and typesetting copyright © Xoum Publishing 2014
Cover design by Xou Creative, www.xou.com.au

National Library of Australia Cataloguing-in-Publication entry

Author:	Falkiner, Suzanne, 1952- author.
Title:	Mrs Mort's madness / Suzanne Falkiner.
ISBN:	9781922057914 (paperback)
Subjects:	Mort, Dorothy.
	Women murderers--New South Wales--Sydney--Biography.
	Murder--New South Wales--Sydney.
	Insanity defense--New South Wales--Sydney.
	Trials (Murder)--New South Wales--Sydney.
Dewey Number:	364.1523099441

Word count 66,000

CONTENTS

Foreword xi
Prologue 1

Part One: The Lindfield Tragedy

1—Ingelbrae, Tuesday, 21 December 1920 7
2—Fidèle à la Mort 19
3—Lindfield, July 1920 27
4—Claude at War 32
5—The Conchologist 46
6—Claude in France 54
7—'The Pyjama Man' 60
8—Claude in London 67
9—Manly in Winter 81
10—Interlude 86
11—To the City 92
12—Ingelbrae, Tuesday, 21 December 1920 97

Part Two: The Investigation and the Trial

13—Claude at Rest 101
14—Miss Fizelle's Nightmare of a Day 103
15—The Investigation 114
16—The Inquest 126
17—The Trial: the First Day 140
18—The Afternoon of the First Day 163
19—The Trial: the Second Day 177
20—The Verdict 191

Part Three: The Aftermath

21—Dorothy Alone 197
22—Mad or Bad? 199
23—In Hindsight 210
24—*The Love Flower* 219
25—Claude at Cricket 222
26—The Death of a Ladies' Man 228
27—The White Poppy 234
28—Outside the Drawing Room Door 240
29—In Long Bay Gaol 248
30—Harold's Secret 268

A Coda 281
Sources and Acknowledgements 287

For Ruth

How many deeds, particularly committed by women that in themselves seem deplorable have become glorified down through history because they were committed in the name of love.

—Opening inter-title from the film *The Love Flower*, United Artists 1920

FOREWORD

Rare in the annals of murder is the crime known mainly by its victim; usually it is the perpetrator who goes on to notoriety and infamy. Dr Claude Tozer, however, secured himself a bizarre renown in cricket when he became one of only a score or so first-class players to meet an untimely, violent end at the hands of another.

Tozer was a good cricketer who might have become better yet. His record suggests a batsman coming into his prime, somewhat delayed by medical studies, and World War I. He had the genes for it. His uncle, on his mother's side, was Percie Charlton, a medium pacer who played two Tests for Australia in England in 1890. He had advantages too, being the son of a successful banker and the nephew of a senior public servant; he learned the game on the verdant ovals of Shore, whose gifted first XI he joined as a precocious fifteen year old, playing alongside the likes of Roy Minnett and Jack Massie.

In four years as a first XI cricketer, Tozer made 2010 runs at 48.87, with six hundreds. In 1907–08, he made 261 against St Joseph's; in a famous game in 1908–09, he contributed 140 to a Shore total of 301, only to see

Sydney Grammar reply with 916, including an innings of 356 by Eric Barbour. Both Barbour and Tozer then pursued medical studies at Sydney University, whose first XI they represented in the Sydney grade competition. For consecutive seasons, 1912–13 (794 runs at 72.2) and 1913–14 (872 runs at 76.55), he was that competition's most prolific player; in the second of those summers, in which University won the pennant, Tozer made three hundreds.

Tozer's priority, however, remained his studies, then his position at Sydney Hospital: he largely abjured interstate cricket, representing NSW with modest success in four matches, none of them in the Sheffield Shield. Then in June 1915, he enlisted in the Australian Army Medical Corps, served in the Dardanelles and northern France, and had a dangerous three years in the colours. He was mistakenly reported dead at Lone Pine; he was stricken with typhoid in Egypt in January 1916; he was blown up at Pozières six months later, and riddled with shrapnel. Nonetheless, in October 1917, he earned the Distinguished Service Order for continuing to dress the wounded and organising ambulance bearers while under heavy fire at Hooge Tunnel near Ypres.

Writers often call Tozer 'dashing', but this is more through what he'd done rather than who he was: he was a steady rather than brilliant cricketer and, it would seem, a conservative man, devoted to his widowed mother. He slotted evenly into the life of a North Shore general practitioner after his discharge in April 1919, and resumed his cricket successfully too, compiling his only first-class hundred six months later at the Gabba against Queensland: 103 in two and a half hours.

Tozer began the following season so brilliantly in grade cricket for Gordon—110, 211 and 131 in consecutive innings—that he was included in an Australian XI to play the visiting England team on the same ground in December 1920. It was a remarkable progression, but endorsed by former Australian batsman Frank Iredale in the *Sun*: 'I don't suppose that at the moment there is a sounder player in the state.' He made a creditable 51 and 53, and appears in a team photograph behind the legendary Australian skipper Warwick Armstrong. Such was his progress that Tozer was nominated to captain NSW in their next home match. Tozer had never allowed cricket to get in the way of his life before; but life was about to get in the way of his cricket, permanently and irrevocably.

Suzanne Falkiner's *Mrs Mort's Madness* is not a cricket book: it is a carefully assembled but highly readable account of a sensational crime. As observed, the crime has hitherto been known by its victim. Nearly a century after it transfixed Sydney, Suzanne has at last rounded the story out.

Gideon Haigh

PROLOGUE

It was the white cockatoo that first led them to the murder, they told me. Or was it the mis-delivered parcel?

I had knocked at their door once before, but the small cottage in the northern Sydney suburb of Lindfield was unwilling to give up its secrets. I had no idea who lived there now, and with a change of street name in the intervening years, I was not even certain I had the right address.

Beyond a cascade of silver North Shore commuters' cars flowing homeward on Tryon Road, I found some disused-looking stone steps, a rusted gate overgrown with shrubs, and a concrete path winding steeply upward. I hesitated at first, unsure of my welcome. Dark blue hydrangeas and drooping palms lent the garden an air of somnolence in the late afternoon, almost of other-worldliness, and so I was not surprised when the old-fashioned electric door bell sounded emptily in the interior and no one responded.

An even narrower path led around the side, but my imagination was already at work and I did not want to be challenged for trespassing. I retreated to my car and made a rough sketch in my notebook: a classic pre-war double-fronted Californian bungalow built on damp sandstone foundations, with a small covered porch and a miniature verandah to the right, its original wooden half-shingles and white-painted timber trim all still intact. Then I walked around by the main road to Owen Street at the back, where my snooping over the fence revealed a more ordinary modern extension and garage. I lingered too long, and a dog began to bark.

When I tried again some weeks later, a teenage girl came to the door and silenced the barking dog to tell me her parents were not at home. I gave her my telephone number. Perhaps they would call me? Research, I said, for a biography. Someone of interest had once lived in the house. I would like to talk to them, and perhaps even to see inside, if they were willing.

Shortly after, sitting on a rose chintz sofa in a drawing room pleasantly cluttered with English porcelain and framed family photographs, I told them what I knew. The house had been called 'Ingelbrae' in the early part of the last century and someone had been murdered here, in this very room. The murderer, a Mrs Mort, had shot her doctor as he sat on her sofa writing a prescription. She was thought to be mad, I added, but I was not so sure.

My host, Bruce, a lean man who had introduced himself as a television producer, received the information with equanimity. 'That would explain the ghost, then,' he said.

His wife, Barbara, was not at all surprised to hear that someone living here had been driven to a desperate act. This part of the road was sunk into a depression between two ridges, and there was never a fresh breeze.

They had already learned something of the house's history from Marjorie, an elderly neighbour. Now in her early nineties, Marjorie had grown up in Owen Street, and remembered as a child walking up to play with her friend at No. 13, opposite, and being 'hurried past' when the bodies were brought out in the morning. At eight years old she was not permitted to ask questions, but she knew from the adult conversation going on around her that it was the doctor who'd been involved. The woman had killed him, she thought, because her child had died and it was his fault.

'But it was not in the morning when the body was brought out,' I said, 'and there was only one.'

Some time after that, added Barbara, when the family was out searching for their lost pet cockatoo, they knocked at a door in Slade Avenue, on the corner near the creek, and discovered another elderly woman who had known the area in its early days. But when they asked about the history of their own house, she was silent. She wouldn't talk about it, she said, 'because of the children still being alive'. At that point Bruce and Barbara knew that *something* had happened, but not exactly what.

A visitor, entering the house, once remarked it had 'something ill-feeling' in it, Barbara went on, and her mother-in-law Vera had several times seen 'a lady in grey' drifting down the passage. Once she had seemed so real that Vera had called out to her, thinking it was Barbara. Vera had already proved prescient—as a child she had foretold the death of a cousin in World War I, long before the telegram came.

Barbara sometimes had the sensation of someone

brushing past her in the hall, accompanied by a strong perfume—an exotic floral fragrance. Their middle daughter, too, when younger, claimed she had seen a little boy peeping out from behind the piano in the smaller bedroom, and wouldn't practise there any more. No one liked being in that room.

I had no comment to make. I don't believe in ghosts, outside the creations of the human mind with all its susceptibilities and suggestibilities, and these ghosts seemed predicated on dubious information. Although, if anyone were likely to linger incorporeally and pester the living, it might very well be Dorothy Mort. But the coincidence of the floral scent unsettled me. I had already envisaged her as wearing a fragrance of tea roses.

Part One

The Lindfield Tragedy

ONE

Ingelbrae, Tuesday, 21 December 1920

Four days before Christmas 1920, at around eleven o'clock in the morning, Florence Fizelle opened the front door of Ingelbrae to Dr Claude Tozer. The previous week's heavy rain had cleared and morning sunlight dappled the street through the grey-green eucalyptus leaves. No doubt they greeted one another politely, but Miss Fizelle saw that Dr Tozer was distracted as he stood on the coloured mosaic tiles beneath the porch. Beyond the garden path, she would testify later, she noticed his motorcar on the grass.

Miss Fizelle's mistress, Dorothy Mort, had been ill, on and off, for weeks. The previous evening her husband, Harold Sutcliffe Mort, had gone next door to telephone for the doctor to attend her in the morning. He had left around 9.00 a.m. to catch his usual train to the city, and Miss Fizelle had helped her mistress tidy her room and put on a fresh nightgown in preparation for the doctor's visit. In the distance she could hear Dorothy's two young children, Poppy and Pat, on holiday from school, playing in the bush down by the creek.

At a little over six feet tall, Claude Tozer towered over Miss Fizelle in the cramped hallway. Despite the warmth of the day he wore a well-tailored woollen jacket and waistcoat over a soft-collared shirt, and a black knitted tie with a gold pin. Below his left cuff was a modern wristlet watch. Handsome, slim and athletic, he carried his doctor's bag easily in his other hand, but today he was drawn and pale—so much so, Miss Fizelle thought, that he looked almost unwell himself. She showed him into Dorothy's bedroom and closed the door.

At around 11.20 a.m., sitting in her small room at the rear of the house, Miss Fizelle was startled by a sharp report that broke the still morning.

'DR TOZER DEAD' and 'LINDFIELD TRAGEDY' ran the banner headlines in the *Sydney Morning Herald* the next day. The previous evening, the paper reported, the body of Claude Tozer had been found in the drawing room of Harold Mort's residence at Howard Street in Lindfield, while Mrs Mort was discovered with a bullet injury to the left breast. The paper also recorded that the police had not been called until late that night. Mrs Mort was said to be unconscious, and too ill to make a statement.

After a lengthy investigation that supplied the press with sensational headlines for months, Dorothy Mort was charged with murder. At her trial in April 1921

she was found to be 'not guilty on the ground of insanity' and imprisoned at the Governor's pleasure. Released from Long Bay Gaol nine years later, she showed no further signs of derangement—and the prison doctor was adamant that she never had.

I discovered the story by chance in the newspaper files in the State Library of New South Wales. Initially, nobody was certain whether Dorothy and Claude had been shot from in front or behind, in what order, and by whom. Printed in the *Daily Telegraph* at the time of the inquest was a smudged photograph of Dorothy Mort. The original appeared to be a postcard-sized studio portrait, folded in half, the right size to fit into a man's wallet, which had then been roughly torn up and thrown into a waste paper basket, according to the evidence. Later the police would piece it together and glue it to tissue paper as a court exhibit.

The photo showed a thin-featured woman with large grey eyes and a wavy mass of dark brown hair tied back in a loose knot. At thirty-five, Dorothy's milky skin and spare bone structure conveyed a certain febrile refinement. Her eyebrows were elegantly pencilled arches, her heavy-lidded eyes outlined with kohl and artificial shadows, while her demeanour seemed deliberately to affect the pose of a star of the silent screen—Theda Bara, perhaps. There was something languid about her, yet highly-strung—a look that verged on melancholy. She had been ill, according to one of the daily papers: a chronic sufferer from nerves, or *neurasthenia*.

'Said to have been a beautiful woman at the time of her marriage', another newspaper confided. 'A well-known North Shore socialite', added the scandal sheet

Truth the day after Christmas. 'A few years ago she took a keen interest in moving pictures', this writer continued, 'and we believe took part in several local productions'. The stage name she used—or 'nom de plume', as Dorothy had put it—was 'Diana Reay'.

Beyond this, the journalists were at a loss.

'Mrs Mort. From a torn photograph found in the room in which Dr Tozer met his death.'
Photo: *Daily Telegraph* 15 March 1921, page 5

In the early 1920s only four female offenders were imprisoned in New South Wales gaols for capital offences. Two had been sentenced for performing abortions or baby-farming—disposing of other women's unwanted babies—while another, Eugenia Falleni, an illiterate working-class woman of Italian descent, had created spectacular headlines by impersonating a man and allegedly killing a woman who had believed Falleni to be her husband. At a time when violent crimes by women were relatively rare, Dorothy Mort was another rarity entirely: an educated, middle-class woman accused of murder.

My own interest in the case, at this point, was peripheral. Harold Mort's sister Eirene had at one time taught art at the Mittagong boarding school I had unwillingly attended. Although long retired by the time I arrived, the legendary 'Miss Mort' still lived with her female companion in an old farmhouse on the frigid basalt slopes of Mount Gibraltar. In addition, not far from the house I lived in now, was All Saint's Church, Woollahra, a cold Gothic vault over which Canon Henry Wallace Mort, Harold's father, had long ago presided. Several of my elderly aunts had been married or buried there.

It was mere curiosity, then, that led me to drive out one winter's day to the State Archives in western Sydney where, in a long-neglected box of Supreme Court depositions from 1921, I found a bundle of small brown paper packets that had once contained Dorothy's trial exhibits. Each was catalogued in black ink, and most were empty. One still held some yellowing chemist's prescriptions dated '1920', but the items from packet No's. 15 and 16—a 'locket' and 'gold brooch'—were missing. Packet No. 17—inscribed 'Things found under the settee'—contained a rusty hairpin and a flattened, ninety-year-old Virginia cigarette, lit but barely smoked. A prescription book was also missing, along with the contents of packet No. 22, a 'bottle supposed to contain laudanum'.

An even smaller packet, unnumbered and folded in half, was briefly annotated 'piece of metallic substance'. Like the one intended to contain the laudanum bottle, it was signed with the name 'J. Ramsay'. Shaking out a shard of distressed metal or geological detritus about half the size of my little fingernail, I remembered from my newspaper reading that Acting Inspector Ramsay was the officer in charge of sending evidence to the Government Analyst for forensic testing. Only then did I realise that what I had rolling around in the palm of my hand was a World War I shell fragment from a remote battlefield in France that had been removed from a man's skull during autopsy.

The account that Miss Fizelle, Dorothy's paid companion and housekeeper, gave of the events of Tuesday 21 December 1920 was to shift substantially over the next few months. Her initial explanation as to what had occurred between 11.20 a.m. in the morning, when she first heard what she thought might be the sound of a gunshot coming from the drawing room, and 9.30 p.m. that night, when the police arrived, was alarmingly vague. That afternoon she had gone next door to telephone Mr Mort in the city, she told the detectives, but the telephone did not work, or the message did not get through. Newspapers offered different versions of her identity, and of her role in the household. Even allowing for the vagaries of the journalists reporting the case, her initial statements to police, to the coronial inquiry, and later again to the criminal court, contained gaps and discrepancies. But these were matters on which no one, not even the Crown Prosecutor, pressed her too closely.

In May 1920, when Harold Sutcliffe Mort had first

moved to Lindfield, he did not have a telephone, although his neighbour did. By June, he had engaged Miss Fizelle—the respectable daughter of a country schoolteacher—to keep his wife company and help with her domestic duties. The death of Dorothy's father a year earlier had caused her such prolonged psychological anguish that Harold had also thought it necessary to call in Dr Claude Tozer to treat his wife for her nerves. Dr Tozer, only recently demobbed from the army, had won the DSO for service in France. A prominent sportsman, he now lived with his widowed mother just over a mile away in the suburb of Roseville.

In the early summer of 1919, Claude Tozer, a tall twenty-nine year old with dark blond hair, strode to the crease at the Gordon Cricket Club in one of his first matches after the War. Wearing well-cut white flannels, his bat tucked high under his arm, his thick canvas pads did not impede his loping stride. A photograph in a sporting newspaper shows him looking thin and prematurely lined and drawn, but undoubtedly attractive, with a piercingly direct gaze. It was said that his great strength was his nervelessness and 'ruthless technical skill'. It was the same sort of meticulous concentration he brought to a delicate operation: every ball its own problem of physics, psychology, even philosophy.

Did Dorothy Mort once watch him from a line of wooden deck chairs behind the picket fence, her slim white-stockinged ankle bobbing at first in *ennui*, as he arrived at the wicket, took a couple of steps up the pitch and prodded it with his bat, before stepping back and taking guard?

'I loved him immediately I saw him,' she would later say.

Dr Claude Tozer at cricket, circa 1919. Photo: *Sun*, 14 March 1920

The journalists were not entirely to blame for the dearth of information about Dorothy Mort in late 1920. Her family, unlike that of her husband Harold, left few traces, so there was little enough fabric with which to make her up. Her paternal grandfather John Woodruff, an English customs officer from Kent, had migrated initially to Nelson in New Zealand, where in 1852 he wed Elizabeth Mackay from County Wicklow, Ireland. Coming to Australia not long after, the couple settled in Portland, Victoria, where their son William John Mackay Woodruff was born in 1857. In December 1884, at St Kilda, William Woodruff—or Mackay, as he was generally known—married 24-year-old Helen Thatcher from Warrnambool, a music teacher. Helen's father, described as a man of 'independent means', may have had higher expectations for his daughter than Mackay Woodruff, by now a peripatetic insurance clerk. Dorothy, the eldest of their three children, was born on 2 November 1885. Three years later she was followed by Olive, and then Ronald in 1891.

By 1897, after a brief sojourn in Tasmania, the family moved to Sydney, and 'Corona', a large house subdivided into flats at Findlay Avenue, Chatswood. While Dorothy attended school in North Sydney, Mackay Woodruff, with a partner called Ernest Bell, set up a fire insurance business in the city. On 20 February 1909, at age twenty-three, Dorothy married Harold Mort at St Paul's Anglican Church in Chatswood. The wedding was a family affair: Harold's father, the Reverend Henry Wallace Mort, conducted the service. Mackay Woodruff stood as a witness, and Dorothy's sister Olive was her only bridesmaid. The women's pages of the *Sun* reported that the bride wore white glace chiffon set off by pearl earrings, the gift of her husband, and a borrowed veil of Limerick lace. With her bouquet of asters, roses and orange blossom, Dorothy carried a white leather prayer book given to her by her new father-in-law. A reception for eighty was held in a marquee in the garden of Corona.

After their honeymoon, Harold and Dorothy moved into a rented dwelling in Bondi Road in Waverley, a crowded thoroughfare of two-storey shops and terraces lined with electrical wires and tram tracks.

The couple shifted house frequently over the following years. In November 1910, while still living at Bondi Road, Canon Mort conducted the marriage of Dorothy's younger sister Olive to Reg Renshaw, a young farmer from New Zealand. By 1912, when their daughter Virginia (also known as Poppy, or Peggy) was born, Harold and Dorothy had moved to a small stone house at 12 Wallis Street, Woollahra, not far from All Saints, where Harold served as a Church warden. Poppy was baptised there in April of that year. By this time Helen and Mackay Woodruff, with nineteen-year-old Ronald, had moved to 'Kyerlah', a picturesque cottage in Crow's Nest Road in North Sydney.

Soon after their second child Maurice—known as Pat—was born in 1915, Harold and Dorothy moved again, this time to Boronia Avenue, Cheltenham, near Beecroft railway station in the city's northwest. Finally, in January 1920, for £1460, Harold began the purchase of Ingelbrae in Lindfield, some six miles to the east, and in early May of that year the couple moved in.

At Lindfield, after ten years of marriage and two children, Dorothy appeared to be suffering from some nameless mental malaise. At a time when such matters—such *aberrations*—were usually kept within the family, only the most trusted of medical advice could be sought. And so it was that Harold confided his anxieties in Dr Tozer.

A short time later, on a winter's day in June 1920, Claude got into his new motorcar in Boundary Street in Roseville and drove along Archbold Road to Lindfield, where for the first time he walked up through the lush little garden to the front door of Ingelbrae. Perhaps it was Dorothy who let him in on this occasion, and led him into the small drawing room off the passage. Softly lit by leadlight windows, with dark wooden doors and an austere chimneypiece set off by plain creamy walls, it was a simply-furnished room. A Chesterfield settee with pale cotton covers stood on a Persian rug, framed by two upright wooden chairs in the Arts and Crafts style. The adjoining dining room, with its own door to the hall, was partitioned off by a low ledge and heavy curtain in a William Morris design—the fashionable Bloomsbury look. On the wall hung a photo portrait in a circular frame and a small watercolour painting.

To make his examination, Claude was no doubt obliged to sit close to his new patient, to take her wrist between his fingers and measure her pulse with his usual cool efficiency. A woman not accustomed to indifference, perhaps she was piqued into trying to charm him. Her books—a collection of poems or a play script; a volume of Sir Arthur Conan Doyle's writings on spiritualism; a shilling romance—on the small oriental brass occasional table might have caught his attention. He might have learned of her passion for amateur dramatics and the modern life of the mind. Dorothy planned to audition for one of the new motion pictures being made locally—a rare pursuit among his suburban patients. They quickly achieved an easy intimacy.

Claude must have noted her admiration. He was, after all, a wounded war hero, a man distinguished by honourable service in a world depleted of young men. Already he was recognised as a sportsman in a country where such are held in high regard. A youthful god, with all the pathos of an injured child, and yet endearing with it, like any young man on the verge of a new life.

And, like any young god, he was less accustomed to loving than being loved.

TWO

Fidèle à la Mort

Over time, I have telephone conversations with several elderly Mort relatives. The first, living in Vaucluse, related by marriage, initially does not want to know. The perception she has arrived at—in the absence of hard facts—is that Dorothy Mort was a despicable woman, man-hungry, deluded as to her own charms, and the ruin of her husband. She considers the love affair with Claude Tozer a figment of Dorothy's imagination.

'There are women like that, aren't there, who fall in love with their doctors?' she says. Nothing is to be gained by dredging it all up, she continues. She is proud of the achievements of her husband's forebears, and besides, she says, much of my information is wrong. She has rung various other relatives and advised them not to talk to me.

My second informant, Margaret, in Newcastle, the daughter of Harold's younger brother Stanley, is impatient with all this retrospective rectitude, and also, no doubt, with being told what to do. She is rather more generous.

'I always heard that Dorothy was very beautiful,' she says.

Her memories of Harold Sutcliffe Mort are of a favourite uncle, tall, benevolent and upright, and much loved by a shy child. He had written funny nonsense poems for her, taken all his young nieces and nephews on expeditions to the beach to collect seashells, and had become quite famous in stamp collecting circles, too, she thought. Not long before his death in 1950, when Margaret was in her early twenties and about to depart for England, she had gone to say goodbye to him. Harold, his hands now crippled by arthritis, had asked her to turn over the pages of his albums for him, so that he could look one final time at his beautiful old English and Empire stamps. To her surprise, the last thing he did before she left was to entrust the precious collection to her.

But when I ask about Harold's appearance, there is a silence at the other end of the line. Then, 'He looked like a Mort,' she says, but can think of nothing further.

Mrs Mort's Madness

Thomas Sutcliffe Mort. Photo: unknown

❧

It was said that if Harold's great uncle Thomas Sutcliffe Mort, while reading the *Sydney Morning Herald* one day at breakfast, had not happened upon the story of a prehistoric mammoth found intact in a Siberian glacier, the idea of shipping refrigerated meat to England might never have occurred to him. And if his initial attempts to export frozen beef carcases had ended in odorous failure, then these were just one of the seeds of industry that eventually made him a wealthy man.

Thomas Sutcliffe Mort had built his imposing

family home, 'Greenoakes', in 1846 on thirteen acres of wasteland at Darling Point, at that time too far out of the city to be fashionable. His younger brother Henry—Harold's grandfather—who had followed Thomas from Manchester, had been managing a cattle station at Moreton Bay in the north when Henry Wallace Mort, his eldest son, was born. Some years later, while Thomas was visiting England, the convict surveyor Edmund Blacket made even more gracious improvements to Greenoakes, adding stained-glass windows and a stone carriageway adorned with the motto 'Fidèle à la mort'. Meanwhile, with his livestock auctioneer's eye to a bargain, Thomas had snapped up a job lot from a British ducal estate—oak furniture, paintings and thirty pieces of armour—to furnish it.

Henry Mort Senior, having come south to keep an eye on his brother's business in his absence, moved his wife Maria—the younger sister of Thomas's own socially prominent wife, Theresa Laidley—and seven children into 'Mt Adelaide', a handsome villa next door to Greenoakes. By this time the shady avenues of Darling Point sheltered a number of these fine houses, with grounds adorned with coral and jacaranda trees and their owners' wooden yachts moored peacefully below on Rushcutters Bay. The English novelist Anthony Trollope, visiting in 1872, described one such estate as 'falling down to the sea, like fairyland', and found the Mort brothers' residences 'perfect'.

With this background, the married life that Harold offered Dorothy a few decades later might have seemed enticing, and his encyclopaedic knowledge of arcane facts, attractive. Harold's pride in his antecedents was palpable: his great uncle Thomas had travelled to Peru to bring back alpacas, and Asia for silkworms and sugar cane. He had helped build the great Hunter River steamboats and the Parramatta railway, along with the cathedral-like splendour of Mort's Dock and Engineering Works at Balmain.

Similarly, if his grandmother Maria had not been shipwrecked off the coast of Brazil, Harold's father Henry Wallace Mort might never have become rector of All Saints in Woollahra. In August 1865, having installed her two eldest sons in a respectable boarding school in England, Maria Mort and her younger children had set sail to return to Sydney. Five weeks later their vessel, the *Duncan Dunbar*, was driven aground on a reef some 300 miles off the coast of South America. As the ship began to break up around them, the passengers watched in horror as three fine horses, thrown overboard to lighten the load, plunged helplessly among the breakers and neighed in terror until they were dragged down by sharks. Below deck, Maria put her children to bed amid shrieking timbers and feared the same fate.

Next morning, however, the passengers and crew were able to quit the hulk by boat for a nearby sandbar where, landing among scuttling land crabs and nesting seabirds, they subsisted on meagre rations and little fresh water for several weeks until a passing ship was able to ferry them back to Southampton. When the news of their survival finally reached Sydney, Henry Mort Senior (who for many months believed his wife and five of their offspring lost at sea) announced he would build a church in thanksgiving. His son Henry, after his ordination in England, was to be its first minister.

Henry Wallace Mort, home again and biding his time as a young curate at Parramatta, rode his horse regularly to Darling Point to watch the masons' progress. In 1876—the same year he married Katie Isaacs, daughter of the colony's first Solicitor General—he delivered his first sermon at All Saints. Selwyn, their eldest son, was born a year later; Harold followed on 9 June 1878; then Eirene and Eunace, and finally Stanley.

Woollahra was a mixed parish. Beyond the great houses and gardens of Darling Point, dirt tracks led between brick-and-shingle workers' cottages around Captain Piper's—later Queen—Street. Roaming between the fishing shacks and Chinese vegetable gardens of Double Bay and Rose Bay's saltwater swamps and paperbark forests, young Harold Mort developed a love of natural history. From his mother Katie, whose married sisters sent her exotic stamps from all over the Empire, he inherited a devotion to philately. This family also moved frequently: it was not until 1897 that they finally settled at 'Trevlyn', their graceful two-storey house with broad verandahs in Ocean Street. Each week the Reverend Mort, impressive in black with a full black beard, rode out on his horse to take services also at Watson's Bay and Vaucluse, before returning to Woollahra for his Sunday dinner.

Harold, initially tutored at home, and with a talent for mathematics, was Dux of his final year at The King's School at Parramatta. By 1901 he had completed a Bachelor of Science at the University of Sydney and—seeing little financial future in becoming a naturalist—begun a course in Mechanical and

Electrical Engineering. All three Mort boys would become engineers: Selwyn in Mining and Metallurgy, while Stanley went to work for the Water Board.

Eirene Mort, a neat young woman with brown plaits wound around her head, took painting lessons with the young Italian artist Dattilo Rubbo before sailing alone for London and the National Art School. Eunace, the musical one, learned pianoforte and violin from Miss May Pettifer, a prolific local composer of patriotic songs and sheet music. In 1905, when Eirene returned to establish an artist's studio with her friend Nora Weston, Eunace also left for London to continue her studies.

Harold, meanwhile, having enrolled in his final year of Engineering in 1904, did not graduate. In January 1907, with his schoolboy brother Stanley and a group of other students, he accompanied his charismatic Geology teacher Professor Edgeworth David on an expedition by horse and bullock dray to explore the Pleistocene landforms of Mt Koszciusko. In a paper to the Linnean Society in 1908, Edgeworth David commended Harold for his survey of the Blue Lake, a glacial landform he plotted from a coracle made of canvas, saplings and rabbit-proof netting. A light-hearted student 'newspaper' documenting the excursion attributed to Harold 'a rather overbearing conceit for his looks, legs, learning and lineage', along with 'a keen appreciation of humour—particularly his own'.

'He takes himself very seriously,' the anonymous correspondent concluded. 'If he could overcome this tendency, his conversation might be more edifying: his jokes are deep, and their point is not always apparent.'

After some ten years as a student, Harold finally graduated in Engineering in April 1908, the year before he married Dorothy. In 1910 he completed a degree in Military Science. Sometime after this, he took a position as a surveyor with the New South Wales Rail and Tramway Department, where he would remain for the rest of his career.

THREE

Lindfield, July 1920

Shireen,
Boundary Street,
Roseville
3/7/20

Dear Lady Diana,

    Permit me just to congratulate you on the exceptionally charming seal you are using. I didn't manage to fathom the crest, but will endeavour to do so at our next meeting. Surely there must be a motto attached—presumably Latin—"Semper Fidelis", or, I hope, something more recherché. Glad to hear you are on the mend, because we can then compare symptoms and mingle tears and sympathies. I am afraid you are responsible for my illness—yes, very compromising, I admit, but, then, how can anyone die better than in such compromising conditions?

    Roads permitting, I shall bring myself and the devil thing misnamed a motor to your front door, or as near as possible, on Tuesday next, for tea. If the roads are too bad I shall proceed "aux pieds", especially to see the costume made by your own clever fingers.

Please don't overdo things at the studio, because I'll let you into a secret. The only ways this influenza kills, apart from the doctor's errors, are—

    1. Going to bed late

    2. Getting up too early

    3. Doing too much too early

Au revoir, and the best of luck with the American producer. Smile on him sweetly and he MUST capitulate—

Yours very sincerely,

C. J. Tozer.

Claude's first letter to Dorothy, written less than two weeks after they first met, was one of four printed in the newspapers during the coronial inquest into his death. His handwriting, in fountain pen, is remarkably legible for a doctor: poised and confident, with generous loops slanted to the right, and saved from any effeminacy by its strong verticals. It is unusually intimate for a doctor writing to a married patient, despite any light-hearted rapport they may have achieved.

Tryon Road today is a densely-crowded rat run, where well-dressed young mothers in black four-wheel drives throng the parking lot at Lindfield village and drink caffè lattes in bistros around the modern shopping centre. Only a handful of the small, canopied Victorian shops remain beside the railway station to mark the earlier settlement, while a few majestic eucalypts still break the skyline above the older houses. The massive red-brick Anglican church of St Albans, rebuilt in 1921, squats in near-antiquity with a brutal modern extension grafted onto the back. On the day I visit, some of the older women of the community have arrived to clean brass and arrange flowers in its dark and ornate interior. None among them, nor those at the local library or historical society, has any knowledge of Dorothy Mort's brief sojourn here.

These further reaches of Sydney's North Shore, once covered by dense tracts of gum forest and steep gorges, were settled long after the more accessible parts of the city. First came the convict timber-getters, hauling out the precious cedar logs by bullock dray and jinker to Fidden's Wharf on the Lane Cove River. Soon their rough camps gave way to the shanties of market gardeners and orchardists, who were quick to sell their rural land grants for housing when talk of the northern railway line began. The last of the great Turpentine trees were cut down for sleepers while the vast sandstone overhangs, often concealing ancient Aboriginal paintings and carvings, were mined for the roadways. By the 1890s, when the railway track from Milsons Point finally reached Hornsby, orderly rows of raw timber fences and telegraph poles were already marching along Tryon Road. By 1920 the subdivision between Howard and Owen Streets—named for its surveyors—was just one of the new, modern developments springing up along the North Shore line. And as a railway surveyor himself, Harold could be proud to call himself part of that progress.

To the north, beyond the new Park and Recreation ground, Gordon Creek still wound in a forested wilderness down to Middle Harbour. At Lindfield village, a brisk half-mile to the west, a miniature post office and string of terraced shops—Nunn's Hardware, Davies' Newsagency, Sinclair the chemist and Duvall's Drapery—clustered around the railway bridge. Private elementary schools for Poppy and Pat lay within walking distance, while the dairyman from Primula Street called twice daily and fresh vegetables could be had from the Chinaman in Treatts Road. Already, foundations for the new Anglican church were in place, and the program of municipal tree-planting and flowerbeds was coming along nicely.

Ingelbrae, a neat five-room cottage on a sloping battleaxe block at 11 Howard Street, stood out prominently as Harold returned from the railway station in the evenings. It was not to be compared to Trevlyn back in Woollahra, even with a fibro extension added as a maid's room at the back, but Harold, at forty-two, was by no means a rich man, and by now had little prospect of becoming one. No doubt he hoped the move to Lindfield would be his last.

Outside Dorothy's closed bedroom door, late at night, Harold might have sat at his specimen table, sorting and labelling the homely chitons and limpets of the Sydney basin, neatly gluing each to a stiff cream card. Next to it, in India ink with a fine-nibbed mapping pen, he inscribed a meticulous notation of genus and species, vulgar or common nomenclature, place and date of collection. This was cross-referenced to his field notebook, where he listed any relevant observations of habitat, diet and method of reproduction.

On his solitary collecting expeditions among the rock pools and weed beds of Middle Harbour, he carried his preserving jars and slides, his glass viewing funnel and his net, his bottles of seventy per cent alcohol and hydrogen peroxide. Perhaps it took him back to the days when a collection of slow-moving starfish and sea urchins, carried excitedly home from Seven Shillings Beach in a child's tin bucket, aroused the fond admiration of his busy but distracted mother and the pleased attention of his upright clergyman father.

Harold Sutcliffe Mort liked to keep nature in order.

FOUR

Claude at War

On a trip to London I take the opportunity to visit the Imperial War Museum off Lambeth Road. Set in formal lawns intersected by geometrical paths and sharply-pruned rose gardens framed by rampant fifteen-inch guns, it is a peculiarly masculine enclave. Tall stone pillars and a gloomy atrium lend a forbidding air, a reminder that up until 1930 this was the Bethlehem Mental Asylum, or Bedlam. Inside, under the domed roof, it is not hard to hear distant echoes of screaming strait-jacketed inmates, forced into daily cold baths or chained howling to the floors. I discover I must pay a £6 entrance fee, having omitted to ring ahead to make an appointment with the library.

'I am looking for the record of an Australian doctor who won the DSO on the Somme,' I say to the man behind the counter at the reference desk.

He looks me over dubiously. 'Are you sure he won it? A lot of people say they won the DSO.'

After some bureaucratic ritual I am escorted to a tiny lift and ascend to a circular Reading Room inside the dome. In this milky-glassed eyrie a few elderly men are buried in piles of archival tomes under the watchful eye of a male librarian at a raised desk. When the relevant indexes are delivered, I find that my Australian source was wrong in its dates, which was why I was unable to locate the record. A *London Gazette* reveals that Major Claude Tozer won his Distinguished Service Order in September 1917 for actions with the 3rd Australian Field Ambulance during the battle of Menin Road.

At Hooge Tunnel east of Ypres, Major Tozer had shown 'a most conspicuous courage and devotion to duty' in dressing the wounded under fire and organising the relief of his Ambulance bearers as far forward as the Regimental Aid Posts just behind the front lines. Working under constant shellfire, his complete disregard of danger and unremitting attention to the wounded was highly praiseworthy. Six weeks later in early November, after his unit had been withdrawn and Claude himself evacuated to the 10th British Hospital at Le Tréport suffering diarrhoea and exhaustion, he had also been mentioned in despatches by the British commander Sir William Haig.

Back home at 'Birkhall', a dark brick cottage at 15 Burroway Street in Neutral Bay, Claude's widowed mother Beatrice Tozer would have read a similar paragraph in the *Commonwealth of Australia Gazette* of 18 April 1918.

Claude's father Jonathan Tozer had joined the Bank of New South Wales in 1873, at age eighteen, and quickly rose from clerk to accountant, first at Head Office in

Sydney and then at Parramatta. Made manager of the St Mary's branch at twenty-six, he was sent to try his mettle in the bush. After eight years of subsisting on boiled mutton and cabbage in public dining rooms and leading a bachelor's existence in bare uncarpeted rooms above the bars of the second-best hotels of Walgett, Gunnedah and Narrabri, he was transferred back to the city.

In 1889, while in charge of the Sussex Street branch, he married 23-year-old Beatrice Charlton, younger of two daughters of Thomas Apedaile Charlton, solicitor, of 21 Cleveland Street, Redfern. Among Beatrice's eight brothers, Leopold and William—the latter of whom conducted their wedding ceremony at St Philip's church in York Street—were ordained Anglican ministers; the others were in banking, dentistry and medicine. A nephew, Andrew Charlton, better known as 'Boy', was soon to become well-known as a swimmer.

Claude was born at 162 Sussex Street on 27 September 1890, the same year that his uncle Percie Chater Charlton played Test cricket for Australia. While his father went on to manage banks at Crookwell, Mudgee and Cootamundra, Claude, at twelve, was sent to board at the Sydney Church of England Grammar School, or Shore, in North Sydney. By age fifteen he was playing in the school's first cricket XI. By his senior year, 1908, as head of school and senior prefect, along with his usual prizes in Divinity and Mathematics, he won his form prize, a general studies prize, the Latin Medal, a special prize for Literature and another for Ancient History, and the Pockley Prize for best all-rounder. As vice president of the Debating Society, begun by an enthusiastic new young English master, Claude argued that the newly-federated Colonies should secede from the Empire, that England's army was superior to her navy, and had put a strong case against military conscription: their British forefathers had never stood for it, Claude maintained, and neither should they. As cricket captain, according to the school's *Torchbearer* magazine, he was the team's hardest batsman to dislodge.

Claude's cricketing ability came to wider attention in March 1909 when he played in the Greater Public Schools (GPS) Competition final at North Sydney Oval. In the face of a massive score of 916 by Sydney Grammar, in a game notable for fielding eight future first-class players, Claude scored 140 of Shore's 311 runs.

In the same year, his first in Medicine at the University of Sydney, among twenty-nine other male students residing within the lofty sandstone walls of St Paul's College, he won the College tennis doubles and a High Distinction in Chemistry. In February 1911, at twenty, he made his first class debut at the Sydney Cricket Ground under captain Victor Trumper. Gaining another high distinction in Fourth Year Medicine, he then dropped back a little in 1914, graduating with only second-class honours.

By this time, Claude had become something of a curmudgeon. As student representative on the College Committee he had earned the nickname 'Auntie'—both for his surly dedication to running the College and his tendency to lodge complaints with the authorities. While acknowledging his outstanding academic and sporting record, the St Paul's magazine also paid fond tribute to 'his sunny disposition and unfailing courtesy'.

His closest friend was Herbert Locksley St Vincent Welch, an older medical student and Shore old boy with whom he shared a study. A handsome, nuggety blond, also a committed scholar and athlete, Welch—whom Claude had 'taken unto him as his wife'—was known to 'smooth and soften' his impetuosities, according to the *Pauline*'s light-hearted banter.

'Together they strode up the straight and narrow path, distributing geniality and goodwill on all comers,' the anonymous writer noted. With a reputation for disdaining frivolous pleasures for long hours of study late at night, the pair were also known for 'their lofty indifference to the weaker sex'.

Claude had yet to complete his residency at Sydney Hospital when war was declared in August 1914. Recruiting began less than a week later. Crowds gathered at noticeboards outside newspaper offices, avid for news of heroic Australian adventures overseas. The lists of casualties trickled through rather more slowly.

In late April 1915, following an urgent call for more medical personnel after the Gallipoli landings, Claude left the Royal Hospital for Women in Paddington and enlisted in the Australian Army Medical Corps. A photograph taken around this time shows a slender, pale young man with a sensitive mouth and apprehensive eyes, whose officer's cap—familiar enough, no doubt, from the school cadets—sits uneasily on his forehead. Weighing eleven stone twelve pounds, at six feet and half an inch tall he cleared the minimum height by a good six inches. A few days after enlisting, Lieutenant Tozer dressed himself in his newly-issued woollen underwear and stiff dark-grey flannel shirt and tie, his khaki jacket and cord breeches and army boots and puttees, and marched out through the cheering crowds in Martin Place to board the coastal steamer *Karoola* for Egypt.

Claude Tozer, Australian Army Medical Corps, circa April 1915.
Photo: unknown

Herbert St Vincent Welch had already left Australia with the 1st Field Ambulance the previous October and was stationed at the tent city on the plain of Mena near the pyramids, five miles west of Cairo. A bleak place, the white dust that blew in from the desert made the drilling Australians resemble a battalion of ghosts, reported war correspondent C.E.W. Bean. Hot and dry in the day, the nights were bitterly cold. Those not already ill with respiratory and eye complaints came down with dysentery, and the medical officers spent most of their time supervising latrines and lecturing the men in hygiene. The nearby Mena Hotel had been taken over for infectious diseases.

The No. 1 General Hospital, to which Claude would be assigned, was in the Palace Hotel at Heliopolis, on the city's northern outskirts opposite the railway line. Within its Edwardian turrets and domes, massive stone colonnades dwarfed thousands of white-draped cots for minor wounds and convalescents. Those with serious wounds were sent to four British military hospitals in Alexandria; in Cairo the Australians cared for the rest. The 1st Field Ambulance's tented division—horses, waggons and the transport section—would remain in Alexandria until they embarked for the Turkish mainland.

At Cannakale, in late May, the landscape is tinged with green, while beyond the pebbled shore the pale aquamarine of the Aegean sea is softened by mist. In the early morning a few of us walk uphill on a winding path towards the high ridge where, a kilometre and a half away, the Lone Pine cemetery is marked by a cenotaph. Heavy black soil clogs our shoes, and spring wildflowers—scarlet poppies, small mauve roses and buttery broom—flourish beside the path. A rangy yellow dog assiduously works the track, mutely inquiring of any newcomer for a hand-out. Halfway up, something overly-symmetrical catches my eye, and I kick out of the compacted mud a corroded iron bung that might once have matched the threads of a metal water tank.

More than ninety years after the invasion, under a silver sky with a splatter of rain, it is easy to see the error made in landing so far up the Gallipoli peninsula. The tilled fields and Lego-land holiday villas further south have given way to forests of squat, windblown pines and terrain too steep and rocky for cultivation. Encumbered with a heavy pack and weapon, the ascent from the beach would be hellish. The towering rock form they called The Sphinx rises above, making a perfect gun emplacement for any defender.

High on the ridge at Courtney's Post, the closest Australian position to the enemy lines, a vestige of trenches remains among the wiry undergrowth. The war cemetery nearby swarms with busloads of young Turks: boys and girls in jeans, photographing each other in front of Ataturk's famous comments of friendship and regret. Even the most demure of the young Muslim women in their hijabs are self-conscious about their appearance. They are friendly, and about the same age as many of the Turks and Australians who died here.

Anzac Cove itself is disfigured by a two-lane highway that now entombs the low-lying tunnels and dugouts where Claude Tozer sheltered on his first night on the mainland. Back down at the beach, the water-washed pebbles shine red and green and grey and black and mottled white, and I pick up a few for a souvenir. It is very quiet, and surprisingly beautiful.

A week after arriving at Heliopolis in July 1915, along with those 1st Field Ambulance personnel who had been left behind in Alexandria, Claude Tozer was ordered in to prepare for the British attack at Suvla Bay of August 6. In the event, these reinforcements were held back on the Greek island of Lemnos until—with Claude among them—they were landed by the trawler *Stonus* on Anzac beach in the pre-dawn hours of August 11.

It was near midnight when the lighter finally nudged alongside to ferry them ashore, another medic reported, and the lap and gurgle of the black water seemed terribly close. Claude Tozer was one of two officers who climbed down a rope ladder into the huddle of subdued nineteen- and twenty-year-old stretcher bearers and orderlies, recruited and trained for a scant two weeks at Queens Park in Sydney. In the distance, lit occasionally by shellfire, the Turkish landmass rose even blacker than the dark sky, and for the first time they heard the clatter of enemy guns. Behind them floated the giant hospital ships, garlanded with red and green lanterns. When the lighter's keel crunched into the shallows and Claude swung his legs over the side, the pebbles shifted under his feet as the seawater filled his boots and rose to his knees.

Above them, in the shelter of the rising terraces, myriad tiny lights indicated where their compatriots were huddled together for warmth and comfort. Then an orderly arrived to lead them to a nest of tarpaulin-covered gullies behind the beach where the medical staff took cover and, spreading their ground sheets and pulling up their greatcoats, they slept intermittently and waited for daylight.

When Claude crawled out into the bright sunlight next morning, the pinpricks of light from the previous night resolved themselves into thousands of half-naked soldiers crawling like semi-subterranean cave dwellers over an arid terrain. Beyond the height of summer, the ochre-coloured hills of Gallipoli had long been stripped of scrub for cooking fires, laying bare a warren of dry wells, trenches, dugouts and sappers' tunnels. By now most of the men, emaciated by dysentery and burnt almost black by the sun, had discarded their uniforms for a pair of boots and ragged shorts, a torn singlet and an improvised turban. Above the cesspits and bloated corpses scattered over no-man's-land buzzed clouds of black flies, while every breeze filled the foetid air with dust.

On the distant ridges, quivering in the heat haze, points of movement marked where the water carriers, trudging with heavy metal tanks on their backs, wound up narrow paths to the front. Turbaned Sikhs goaded strings of mules along other near-perpendicular tracks. From the higher points, hidden nests of Turkish snipers and artillery kept the occupied strip below under constant fire. Beyond the concealed burrows of the medical headquarters, and the sheltered hospital tents and piles of mule fodder on the beach, a motley collection of barges and horse boats butted against each other in the glassy water.

From the 1st Field Ambulance Lieutenant Tozer was assigned almost immediately to ANZAC headquarters, where Colonel Neville Howse, the chief medical officer, was trying to disentangle the logistical chaos following the disastrous earlier attacks. A fortnight later, in late August, Claude was transferred to the 3rd Field Artillery Brigade of the AIF. In the next few weeks, at some improvised collecting post between the frontline and the beach, he would undergo a rapid and brutal initiation into field medicine, assessing and treating the wounded and passing them up or down the evacuation line. During August the onshore medical teams worked twenty hours a day, performing little else but emergency surgery, and with little time for rest.

Following a rumour that he had been killed in the Dardanelles shortly after his arrival, a 2nd Field Ambulance orderly wrote back to Sydney headquarters that Claude was still alive, and fit. He knew the Lieutenant well by sight, he reported: a tall young man, of medium complexion, and fresh looking.

A photograph in the Australian War Memorial from around this date shows four uniformed young officers off-duty at Courtney's Post, the closest point to the Turkish lines. Loosely ranged against a wall of sandbags, with eyes half-closed as if in amusement at some private joke, they look like schoolboys who have managed to climb the highest tree on offer without being caught. Claude, in shorts, leggings and a sun helmet, wears a white armband with a red cross on his tunic sleeve and sports a weedy moustache. He had just turned twenty-five.

Mrs Mort's Madness

Captain Claude Tozer AAMC, far left, standing just behind the trenches at Courtney's Post, Gallipoli, August 1915.
Photo: Australian War Memorial

Sometime later he appears in the collection again, looking on as Major Hugh Poate, also from Sydney University, barbers the hair of Colonel Howse. Poate, in shirtsleeves and braces, rests his hand almost affectionately on the older man's balding skull, while Howse submits his towel-draped head to the steel clippers. Claude stands to one side, chatting to his commanding officer, whose eyes are also creased with laughter. Claude's uniform jacket is now noticeably stained and battered, and the buttons strain across his chest. In his hand, held soldier's fashion, is a lit cigarette, shielded by his palm. The three men seem perfectly at ease with each other, despite the differences in age and rank. Wires pass overhead, and the steep scrubby hill behind them is littered with crates and piles of equipment.

By autumn, however, a certain monotony had set in, although the deadly gunfire was constant. Fresh water remained scarce, and mail still wasn't getting through. Claude's last letter to his parents, care of the Bank of New South Wales in Cootamundra, had been in mid-September, after a brief leave on Lemnos, where they had scrounged in the windswept Greek villages for eggs and fruit and honey, a rare respite from salt beef and hard biscuit.

On 5 October Claude was photographed again with twenty-six other Royal Army Medical Corps officers after a lecture from the prominent British surgeon Sir Victor Horsley on the effects of gunshot wounds to the head. The men, idling in small groups, are mostly unaware they are being observed; some are already walking back down the rocky path to the beach. Major Poate stands above them on a hillock overlooking a cluster of stained tents lashed to a rubble-and-sandbag reinforced ledge. Claude, in his sola topi and distinctive white armband, is looking up into the sun, towards the photographer. Despite the cooler weather he still wears his baggy khaki shorts, but retains the formality of his officer's dark grey shirt and tie. Once again he holds a cigarette between thumb and forefinger, cupped in his palm. Against his chest, tucked in a tunic pocket, will be a tiny tin of Vespa wax matches.

At home, rumours of Claude's death persisted. A telegram dated 18 October to the Defence Department from a doctor in Cootamundra queried his status. A newspaper reported that the University of Sydney cricket team had worn black crepe armbands in his memory, while the University flag flew at half-mast, but later confirmed that the story was false.

As winter drew on, the men, some wearing homemade jerkins of rabbit-skin against the biting wind, attended Claude's morning sick parades to show their frostbite-blackened limbs. In November a heavy rainstorm washed out an area of shallow graves and flooded the lines with putrefying bodies. Within days it began to snow, and the soldiers turned their rifles skywards as vee-formations of ducks migrated overhead from Russia.

In late December, as a thin line of evacuation ships finally steamed for Egypt, Claude—now Regimental Medical Officer to the 12th Infantry Battalion—spent a frigid Christmas under canvas on the gaunt harbour at Mudros Bay on Lemnos, along with ninety-five nurses from the 3rd Australian base hospital. In mid-February 1916, racked with fever and diarrhoea, he was transferred back to his starting point, the marble halls of the Palace Hotel at Heliopolis. For the fortnight that he lay under its vast chandeliers recovering from paratyphoid, his pay of fifteen shillings per day—remitted direct to Beatrice Tozer's Cootamundra bank account—was reduced to seven shillings and sixpence.

In March, when the Hospital finally closed and the last few patients were evacuated, Claude re-joined the 12th Battalion at Serepeum. At the end of the month, in railway boxes marked *wagon pour 8 chevaux ou 40 hommes*, they left for Alexandria, where the troop ship *Corsican* waited to carry them to France.

FIVE

The Conchologist

By July 1920, twice a week in the evenings, Dorothy would hurry from the ferry landing at the Spit to her drama class in Seaforth. Her teacher, Lily Rock Phillips, lived at 173 Clontarf Crescent on Seaforth Bluff, a spectacular outcrop of rock jutting into Middle Harbour. In this theatrical setting, on a small stage in her living room at 'Nelma', Mrs Rock Phillips—a handsome grey-haired woman of fifty—rehearsed her pupils in a drawing room sketch about a love triangle.

Each evening, as Dorothy heard the snapping sound from the child's toy cap pistol used a prop, she would cross the platform and drop gracefully onto her lover's body. Her stage husband, still holding the pistol, would stare at her as if in horror, and then turn and exit left.

'And again,' Mrs Rock Phillips might say in her modulated tones.

And again Dorothy's 'husband' would walk onto the wooden platform and hand her the gun to load.

From this distance, and from the few photographs that survive, it is hard to be entirely fair to Harold Sutcliffe Mort. Portraits of his more famous relatives show tall, serious, angular-looking men endowed with somewhat horse-faced good looks, but none of them seem enlivened by wit. A lone obituary in the journal of the NSW Royal Zoological Society of 1950 is equally unhelpful. 'For over thirty years a highly respected officer of the Railway and Tramway Department', it offers. As the Society's chairman, and one of the oldest members of its Marine Zoological section, Harold was always willing to pass on his technical knowledge to less experienced collectors.

The only other indication of his character lies in the antique wooden drawers of the old Mitchell Library card catalogue where, in fading ink, his scientific papers are listed. In 'Superheaters and Superheated Steam', delivered to the Sydney University Engineering Society in late 1904, when Harold was twenty-six, he had delivered a spirited treatise on the industrial advantages of pressurised water vapour.

In 1913, four years into his marriage and not long after the birth of Poppy, he had composed 'Transitional Curves for Tramways'—with copious footnotes—on the art of attaining maximum efficiency in the practical applications of the steam engine. In 1923, two years after the events of December 1920 had turned his life on its head, he wrote a further 6000-word discourse on 'Compensation of Grades on Railway Curves of Australia, with Bibliography and Discussion'.

When the Great War came Harold had not enlisted in the regular army—perhaps he was too old, or in a protected industry—although later, after twenty-four years as a volunteer with the University Scouts, a body for training military officers and cadets, he would accept a long service medal from the Governor General.

In July 1928 he shows up again in the records of an expedition to the Barrier Reef in Queensland, studying coral formations near Port Douglas with Professor Edgeworth David and a visiting party of British scientists. Sunburnt and clad in faded shorts, he stands in front of a bleached white tent that shelters a canvas specimen tank. With the sun glinting on his balding pate and his bushy eyebrows forming a hawk-like vee, it is probably only the glare that makes him look severe. Harold was notoriously shy of the camera: this is the only photograph of him that can be found.

Left to right, Harold Sutcliffe Mort, Tom Iredale and Arthur Livingstone at the Australian Museum encampment, Great Barrier Reef Expedition, Low Islands, Queensland, 1928. Photo: Mattie Yonge presentation album, National Library of Australia, Bib ID 3991154

Mrs Mort's Madness

❦

By age twenty-seven, as the eldest daughter, Florence Fizelle was no longer required stay home and housekeep for her family. A position in a respectable household would offer financial independence, even a new social circle. Evidently no suitable marriage prospect had presented itself: young men were in short supply when the war ended.

'Teachers,' a Fizelle relative told me when I inquired about the family background. 'And preachers. Of the spotted wildcat variety.' The few photos he had revealed little of Florence's personality, and he knew of no family anecdotes that attached to her. The first, taken early in the 20th century, shows the four brothers and four sisters standing in front of a faded weatherboard building. Florence, a sturdy country girl with a plain face and a broad chin, is sensibly dressed in a dark blouse, flat shoes and a long white pinafore, her hair tucked under a cloth hat. The other siblings—in aprons and holding mixing bowls and other kitchen implements—all mug for the camera.

The second, more formal portrait, is taken with two of her sisters. The younger girls are almost frivolous, their hair arranged in elaborate curls as if for a party, their identical white lawn blouses ruffled at cuff and collar, each pinned with an outsize posy of cottage flowers. Florence wears a much simpler blouse, and stands with her hands behind her back. Her own nosegay is pinned on lopsidedly to her breast, and her thin brown hair is plainly arranged. She looks at the camera with an expression bereft of artifice.

Florence Fizelle, top right, circa 1915. Photo: Fizelle family

Florence's grandfather George Fizelle had left Ireland in 1852 for the Victorian goldfields, where he stood on a stump at Eagle Hawk near Bendigo to preach the gospel in thanksgiving for his safe arrival after three months at sea. Then, finding no gold, he fell back on his horticultural roots and grew fruit trees and tomatoes at White Hills.

Brother George's religious bloodlines went back to the Palatinate in Southern Germany, from where, in 1709, some 700 devout Lutheran families had found asylum in Ireland through a Protestant immigration scheme. The Fizelles (originally Feacil, or *Fishell*), from Essenheim, had settled with other tight knots of farmers and fishermen in County Limerick. When the evangelist John Wesley passed through in 1745, many became staunch Methodists. Stern, abstemious and industrious, by the early 1800s the German language had died out among them. Half a century later, when waves of Irish immigration flowed to the New World, many of the Palatines went too. In Bendigo, George Fizelle—photographed in later life as a snowy-bearded patriarch in a long black overcoat—continued his Methodist lay preaching for fifty-four years, until he died of influenza in 1906.

Brother Fizelle's only son, Hubert George Fizelle, became a country schoolteacher and migrated north to Albury, Jerilderie, Culcairn and Batlow, steering clear of the cities as places of sin, my informant told me. In 1888, at Balranald in southern New South Wales, he married Agnes Marsden, who taught his pupils needlework. Their daughter Florence was born in December 1893 while her father was stationed at a one-room bush school at Baw Baw, a tiny settlement outside Goulburn. All their children but Florence became teachers. Heather, one of the twins, was the only other of the four daughters not to marry.

When the War came, three of Florence's brothers went. Sergeant Hubert Vere Fizelle, of the Seventh Battalion, was wounded twice at Gallipoli. Sergeant Reginald Cecil Grahame Fizelle—previously an art teacher with the NSW Education Department—was rejected four times before enlisting in January 1916, and was also badly wounded, at Pozières. Geoffrey was a private in the A. Corps Workshops. Kenneth, the youngest, died aged sixteen at Adelong in April 1917, when he laid a loaded shotgun against a wire fence and it went off as he climbed through.

Florence didn't receive the same education as her

siblings. At ten she had suffered from rheumatic fever, and was never robust. Later she became unpaid housekeeper to her family. She, also, was artistic, but found little outlet for her talent, though she won prizes for her painting and photography at country shows. Her father, said my informant, would have nipped in the bud any romance that interfered with her domestic duties, and there was no soldier sweetheart who did not come back from the War. Then, as her younger siblings married or left home to lead independent lives, Florence also set out to find paid work.

Her life remained a mystery after she left. According to her relative, who believed she had been married and divorced, she was footloose. Her parents might have disapproved of her later situation, he thought—Hubert Fizelle was kind, but he was also a strict old time schoolmaster.

But most of this I would not find out until long afterwards.

GET INTO THE MOVIES

MISS LILY ROCHEFORT (Mrs. Rock Phillips),
late of the George Rignold and J.C. Williamson Companies,
has opened **AN ACADEMY** for the teaching
of **DRAMATIC ART** and **PICTURE ACTING**.
Her wide dramatic experience, coupled with her most
successful appearances in the well-known
local productions, "The Pioneers," "Australia's Peril,"
and the Reg. L. ("Snowy") Baker big success,
"THE ENEMY WITHIN,"

and the J.A. Lipman star film, "Just Peggy," &c.,
are guarantees of her ability to impart
the requisite knowledge.

SCREEN APPEARANCES ASSURED.

HIGHEST REFERENCES AS TO BONA FIDES.

For full particulars re sessions and terms, write:—
Miss LILY ROCHEFORT
112a KING STREET
SYDNEY

—*The Green Room*, January 1918

※

On good days, Dorothy would take her children to one of the new picture palaces—the Orpheum in the city, or Traynor's at Roseville—or sew her costume and rehearse her lines, script in hand, walking up and down the small verandah at Ingelbrae, gracefully practising her movements.

Some years earlier she had met a young Englishman, a vagabond writer and actor by the name of Ralph Stock. She had read his stories in *The Lone Hand*, a popular monthly sold for a shilling at the bookstall at Circular Quay. His stirring tales of voyaging in the South Seas, of adventures on the frontier of the Americas, had inspired in Dorothy a belief that she too might do something wonderful with her life.

But eventually Stock had returned to the sea, as all wayward sailors eventually do, and left Dorothy behind in Lindfield.

SIX

Claude in France

In the late afternoon of 5 April 1916 the 12th Battalion disembarked from the *Corsican* at Marseilles amid regimental bands and shouting children and aproned housewives waving from doorways, and marched on cobbled streets to a train that would carry them north to the Somme. Rattling through the city outskirts at dusk, they looked out on blossoming orchards and neat French farms that were the envy of the young, hard-scrabble country boys among them. Then, after three nights of sleeping on hard wooden seats as the train moved inland in a jerky, uneven crawl, the mild weather gave way to rain and cold, the country became flatter and poorer, and the stone farm houses meaner and smaller. Now the children who crowded around their halts begged in broken English for biscuit and cans of bully beef. In place of their sweat-stained felt hats they were given steel helmets and gas masks.

At Sailly-sur-la-Lys the spring weather returned, and they settled in for twelve weeks to drill and train. Here, billeted amid fields of ripening wheat under a lark-filled sky, as enemy reconnaissance planes and balloons patrolled overhead, Claude enjoyed even the smallest of pleasures: the feel of hot water in baths converted from an old civilian laundry at Bac Saint-Maur; the luxury of clean, new-issue garments against his skin. As the daily drill went on, for a brief respite he had little to do but tend the sore feet of men unaccustomed to the stony French roads after the softer sands of Egypt.

In mid-July they shifted south again by rail, and moved out at dusk from a deserted hamlet near Amiens. At their next billet—a cluster of unlit barns and empty stables of wattle and daub—they halted for four days. In the town square of Albert, reached on the evening of 19 July, a moonlit gold-leafed statue of the Virgin loomed from the ruined bell tower as if to offer her child to the men passing silently below. The following day they marched out along the Bapaume Road, past more obliterated farm cottages, moving aside for convoys of British soldiers coming in the other direction. Now, within a few miles of the front, as the muzzle flash of guns pricked the horizon and the artillery barrage grew louder, Claude saw unburied in older trenches his first stiff, grey-uniformed bodies of German dead.

The evening of the 20th brought them in mute single file to a series of shallow, newly-dug incisions zigzagging among ghostly shell craters that pocked the chalky clay. After recent rain, their orderly's torch revealed a pit floor alive with frogs and field mice swimming frantically against the sides. The men who had arrived before them had already excavated sump holes to drain the fouled water, and now they also burrowed in, wrapping themselves in their damp greatcoats to sleep. Shellfire, passing overhead towards the German lines, continued intermittently for most of the night.

※

On the morning of 21 July 1916, Claude woke to a strange silence. Beyond the waterlogged sandbags, as the mist lifted, the rising sun revealed a tangle of wire netting and churned-up shell holes in the middle distance. Through his binoculars he saw the bloated bodies and half-clothed skeletons of British soldiers who had crawled into them and died there, unable to be retrieved.

Beyond these, on the old Roman road between the towns of Albert and Bapaume, a line of pink and white roofless walls marked the ruins of the village of Pozières, with its distinctive windmill. From the German trenches, some 500 yards away, came an occasional wisp of smoke from a cooking fire; otherwise there was no activity. The British had unsuccessfully attacked four times in the past week; now it was the Australians' turn. Under the cover of heavy artillery, advancing with hand grenades and rifles against machine-gun fire, their orders were to take the front line of enemy trenches, and then, at intervals, press forward to the village itself and dig in. Claude's battalion, the Twelfth, would go in with the second wave.

The following morning, 22 July, the men played cards, smoked, wrote home, examined the seams of their clothes for lice, and waited. Then the barrage began, with clouds of suffocating dust, shaking the ground and deafening their eardrums and further fraying their nerves. Finally, at 12.28 a.m. on 23 July, the 1st and 3rd Brigades of the Australian First Division picked up their rifles and went jog-trotting into the darkness.

Claude, a few feet underground in a roofed-over dugout half a mile behind the front lines, briefed his orderlies and checked his supplies. His field tools were simple enough: sharp scissors to cut away a blood-sodden uniform; a good stock of dressings and boiled water; morphia solution and syringes. His primary job was to rapidly stabilise each case—to staunch bleeding, splint fractures, ligature severed arteries, douse open wounds with antiseptic and bandage them—before moving the patient on to the next collecting post. The stretcher bearers bought in the first of the injured just before dawn, and soon he lost all sense of time passing.

Nevertheless, in the back of his mind the overall plan would have remained clear. From the next post—a sniper-ridden junction known as Casualty Corner—motor ambulances were to carry the wounded to a larger dressing station where a team of medics sifted out the dead and dying, methodically redirecting surgery cases and tagging injured men like parcels, white or red, before sending them on down the evacuation line to merge with a larger stream moving in slow convoys by hospital train, charabanc or barge on the Somme to the British hospital at Rouen. From there, his briefing told him, hospital ships would transfer the most serious cases to England, either to be eventually returned to the front or invalided home.

In the chaos and din of the bombardment, however, there was little evidence of that orderly design. The flare of the acetylene lights cast dancing shadows on the walls so that everything seemed to move under his hands, forcing the orderly to hold his kerosene lamp close to the stretcher set on four-by-fours they used as a dressing table. The noise was constant, damping the screams of men who groaned and cried out as Claude attempted to clean their wounds of foetid earth, filthy cloth, fragmented equipment and shards of whatever projectile had brought them down. All around him in the dugout more mud-covered bodies waited: haemorrhaging, mutilated, quivering, helpless. With daylight, only the quality of the darkness would change as the shadows seeped to floor level.

And still, endlessly, the stretcher bearers brought them in.

When the shell landed on top of them the earth walls juddered and the air seemed to writhe about and the two small exploding fragments of hot metal that ended their random trajectory in Claude's skull and right thigh dropped him instantly and soundlessly. After a moment of deafening vacuum the roof and sides of the dugout came raining down, half-burying medics and wounded alike. Four injured soldiers and a field ambulance sergeant died in the blast, along with some German prisoners. The MO and orderly working on either side of Claude, while shocked and concussed, were untouched. Those of Claude's team who were still conscious made feeble efforts to dig themselves out of the debris, until bearers from another aid post arrived to excavate them.

Claude knew nothing of this. No doubt an MO

applied a perfunctory field dressing and turned away to deal with those he thought he could save. Later, someone noticed that Claude was still alive and moved him back into the evacuation line. Unconscious for two days, he was loaded onto a jolting truck and then a train for Calais. On 16 August, ten days after the incident, the HS *Dieppe* carried him to Folkestone. From there, another clattering rail journey terminated in an island of dim light under the arched roof of Waterloo Station, where a roaring crowd, corralled behind ropes and patriotically waving flags, pressed towards a stream of stretcher cases flowing through to waiting motor ambulances.

In August, Claude's father received a letter advising that Captain Tozer had been returned to England with a gunshot wound to the leg. The *University of Sydney Medical Journal* of October 1916 reported that Claude, attached to a mixed regiment of South and West Australians, had been injured in his frontal sinus while working in Captain Eric Fisher's Aid Post.

'Fragment entered the left inner canthus and passed into the right temporal lobe of the brain apparently close under the skull (x-ray finding),' recorded a Medical Board at the 3rd London General Hospital at Wandsworth on 4 September. Also noted was a wound in the right popleteal space. Shrapnel had been removed from his right thigh, but the head wound was left alone, his examiners wrote. No brain lesion was evident, and in the interim the injury had largely healed.

SEVEN

'The Pyjama Man'

Florence Fizelle watched in silence as Harold and Dorothy went their separate ways. This was not the way a marriage was meant to be, she knew from the example of her parents, the two halves of a biblical whole, indivisible under the authority of the patriarch. Unnoticed, she observed her mistress dressing herself in her most striking apparel, putting up her hair in a lustrous corona and applying her lipstick with extra care, before hurrying off to her acting lesson or to the motion picture studio.

Harold had not entirely spelled out to Florence her duty, but she knew the value of discretion. His wife must not spend too much time alone. On those days when Dorothy sank into one of her dark pits of despond, or became bedridden with some nameless malady, Florence must watch carefully over her.

❧

In late 1910, while Harold and Dorothy still lived in Bondi Road, Ralph Stock had disembarked a tramp steamer at Woolloomooloo and walked up Cathedral Street towards the city. A slight, sandy-haired Englishman, the son of a prolific London publisher, he had first left England after seeing a newspaper advertisement recruiting young men to be cowboys and lumberjacks in Canada. Ten years on, from San Francisco Bay, working below decks by way of Honolulu, Fiji and New Zealand, he arrived in Sydney penniless on the eve of his twenty-ninth birthday.

After a night spent beneath newspapers under the Moreton Bay Fig trees in the Domain, Stock had collected his cardboard suitcase from a left luggage depot near the docks and visited a newspaper office in George Street. The editor, spinning in his revolving chair, sorted through a bundle of Stock's photographs of Canada and offered to buy twenty. And could Stock supply letterpress to go with them?

So began Stock's career as a freelance journalist in Sydney. Each day, from cheap lodgings in Darlinghurst, he took a tram to Double Bay or Watsons Bay where, between swims in the harbour's seawater baths, he wrote articles for thirty shillings per thousand words. At the surf carnival in Manly he watched a local girl dressed as Venus rise from the waves and be carried along the beach on a giant conch shell on wheels. With brass bands, cheering crowds and waving flags all day, and at night more bands and people wandering the Corso in everything from pyjamas to evening dress, he wrote, the lack of inhibition was infectious.

At summer's end, in response to a blackboard advertisement outside an Elizabeth Street employment agency, he took a job as a boundary rider on a cattle run near Mt Kosciuszko. Moving between five corrugated iron huts with rough stone fireplaces and sleeping on chaff bags slung between eucalyptus saplings, he spent the winter rounding up stray yearlings and mending fences. Inside each hut, black-and-white illustrations from the *Worker*, the *Sydney Mail* and the *Bulletin* papered the walls. In camp No. 2, three of these were by Norman Lindsay; in No. 4, there were five. At night, while icicle-laden branches creaked outside and the Snowy River ran in a tunnel of ice, Stock smoked his pipe and wrote. One evening, so faint as to be almost inaudible, he caught the strains of a waltz, carried on the wind from the distant ballroom at the Kosciuszko Hotel. When summer came round again, he returned to live in Manly.

In September 1911, Stock's first Australian short story appeared in *The Lone Hand*, edited by Norman Lindsay and A.H. Adams. From June to October his novella *The Recipe for Rubber: a Romance of the South Pacific*, illustrated by Lindsay, was serialised in the same magazine. An author photo accompanying the last episode shows Stock wearing a smart city hat and a racy moustache. When the New South Wales Bookstall Company published the novella in paperback in 1912, the jacket, also drawn by Norman Lindsay, showed a voluptuous girl and a handsome young man carrying a pistol on a tropical beach.

The Recipe for Rubber: a Romance of the South Pacific by Ralph Stock, N.S.W. Bookstall Co, Sydney 1912. Cover by Norman Lindsay. Photo: by permission of the Lindsay Estate

Stock's second novel, *The Pyjama Man*, drew on material from his own life combined with a generous dash of invention. An impoverished young Englishman called Sprague, in previous lives a sheepherder in Montana and a bit-part actor in Washington, is wiling away the summer months in a seaside cottage set among ti-trees at Queen's Cliff, near Manly. Surrounded by a clutter of photographs, sheet music and mementoes of travel, he spends his days in his pyjamas, writing a play on an old typewriter. At night, as the ferry lights ply back and forth from Circular Quay, he tries out lines aloud: a cuckolded husband dramatically threatening his wife's lover with a candlestick, for example.

In the same novel, Sprague meets a dark-haired local girl, Meg, who introduces him to an older woman, 'Nina', later revealed to be a famous actress living incognito. Nina comes to the cottage for tea, served on a cheap tin tray, and reads his work. The actress and struggling playwright recognise each other as denizens of a more jaded European world, and Nina (who rather fortuitously is about to launch her own theatre company in London), offers to produce his play. Sprague and Nina—'a tall, refined-looking woman with a mass of suspiciously auburn hair'—embark together on the liner *Orontes* for England, while Meg, painfully jealous, is left behind.

Sixteen-year-old red-headed Lily Flanagan, a Dublin-born fitter's daughter, had travelled some distance from her origins to get her start in Sydney in 1887. As 'Lily Rochefort' she was an instant success on the stage at Her Majesty's Theatre, the English entrepreneur George Rignold's new crimson-and-gold extravaganza near the Haymarket. Two years later, putting up her age to twenty, she had married Rignold's young property master, George Phillips. At this time both gave their address as Nithsdale Street, a narrow lane at the south end of Hyde Park leading into the slums of Surry Hills.

The couple lived in Balmain and Bondi Junction until around 1907, when Lily and her husband—now calling himself George Rock Phillips—joined the J.C. Williamson's Company just as the famous old theatrical outfit entered the world of silent films. In the years before World War I, when American talking pictures had not yet swamped the cinemas, the industry prospered. By 1912 Lily and George had bought Nelma at Seaforth—named, not as many believed, for Nellie Melba, but for their two daughters, Nellie Rose and Alma, now also beginning their careers as screen actresses. Audiences still thronged to locally-made newsreels, documentaries and dramas, and film-making remained a family affair for the Rock Phillipses.

In 1915 Lillian and Alma appeared in *For Australia*, a patriotic J.C. Williamson production based on the Australian Expeditionary Force's exploits in the Pacific. George Rock Phillips, listed as art director, played the leader of a German spy ring. That year, too, Lillian featured as Alma's mother in an adaptation of Katharine Susannah Prichard's novel *The Pioneers*. Over the next five years, Lily appeared in four more productions, two of which also featured her husband. Alma and George played together or separately in a further five.

By the last years of the War, however, Lillian was nearing the end of her viability as a leading actress, even as screen mother to her real-life daughters. In January 1918, soon after *The Green Room* proclaimed the opening of 'Lily Rochefort's picture academy' in King Street, her first advertisement for acting pupils appeared. Soon after, a 'Screen Contest' was announced. Mrs Rock Phillips's credentials guaranteed her students parts in upcoming films, the magazine reported, and applicants were numerous.

By early May Lillian's classes were obliged to move to larger premises.

These 'larger premises', at 173 Clontarf Crescent, no doubt also represented a major saving in rent. As well as the feature film in which her pupils were to make their debuts, Miss Rochefort also rehearsed stage sketches. At Nelma, with its wide verandah set a hundred feet above the sea, a high-ceilinged salon was furnished with two pianos and a small stage built into a bay window. This little theatre was already well known for private theatricals produced by J.C. Williamson's staff, and the terraced garden below, adorned with rakish plaster statues left over from stage sets, was notorious among the neighbours for scandalous parties attended by 'arty people'.

EIGHT

Claude in London

In late August 1916 the Wandsworth Hospital was mercifully quiet, except for the muted noise of traffic—ordinary Battersea motor traffic—outside the high arched windows. In the hours before dawn, Claude's mind drifted back to Crookwell, Mudgee and Cootamundra, where the wattle and jacaranda trees floated in dream-like colour and the long, hot summers passed in a whirr of grasshoppers and the *cark* of crows. He might recall country town cricket matches played on dry grass, and picking bindi-eyes from a hand-knitted woollen sweater while the local women served tea from a big metal pot with home-made raisin scones and fruit cake under a eucalyptus tree. In an imposing red-brick building in the main street, behind a long red cedar counter, his father in his waistcoat sat in an office smelling faintly of dust and linoleum. Jonathan Tozer's profession would have held Claude a little apart from his fellows in the local schoolyard. A rank above the shopkeepers, and somewhere between the local doctor and the shire councillors, a country bank manager was privy to all the town's secrets.

Then, as an only child, several times a year Claude made the long solitary rail journey back to the coast, clanking laboriously through dun-coloured paddocks of ringbarked trees and huddles of scrawny sheep that darted off awkwardly, tripping over themselves in panic as the train passed. He remembered the sidings where the brass-padlocked navy canvas mail bags were thrown on and off, while the water in the heavy glass bottle in the bracket above rocked in a cloudy prism, until the day-long crawl over plains and mountains ended at his aunt Mary's house at 11 Bennet Street in Neutral Bay. Until finally the hours and years of crowded loneliness in a boarding school dormitory were replaced by the smaller bedrooms, cold showers and erratic bath heaters of St Paul's College. In the exam room and to the rattle of applause from the pavilion, always he had done what was expected of him.

※

There were more recent memories. During those last weeks of routine drill with the 12th Battalion in the desert beyond Heliopolis, a stretcher bearer recorded, the enlisted men had roped their RMO into a camp equitation class. They had watched with glee as Claude's borrowed Light Horse, frantic with delight at the feel of solid earth beneath its hooves after weeks on a rolling troop deck, bolted for the horizon.

Another soldier of the Battalion wrote of lounging on the dock at Alexandria, idling away the last hours as their equipment was loaded onto the *Corsican*, when an Arab urchin solicited their gaze. Dressed in a cut-down digger's uniform, equipped with a scaled-down .303 carved from wood, he had faultlessly wheeled and presented arms, assiduously mimicking their parade drill. No matter what obscure command the soldiers shouted, he obeyed with a smart salute. When some wag invented an order that did not exist, he stood to attention in mute reproach. Then, just as they started to tire of it, like a small automaton he circled the group, wordlessly collecting their tossed piastres in his miniature slouch hat.

In early September 1916, as summer became autumn, Claude was transferred from Wandsworth to the 4th Australian Auxiliary Hospital at Welwyn in Hertfordshire, where a few weeks later he turned twenty-six. In October he was moved to the 2nd Auxiliary Convalescent Hospital at Southall, in South London, where the most severely injured awaited evacuation to Australia.

At Southall, the double amputees skimmed like water-spiders across the polished floors from bed-leg to door-jamb with strapped-on cushions. Men with hideous facial reconstructions roamed the corridors. Outside in the wintry grounds, the walking cases tried to adapt to their new prosthetic devices. With pinned trouser legs and balanced on crutches, crippled nineteen- and twenty-year-olds negotiated the frozen wastes between one hospital building and another. The ground was covered with icy slush and it was dark by four in the afternoon.

'Says he is well, but still pale and does not look robust', reported Claude's Medical Board on 23

October, marking him still unfit for service. By November, four months after he was wounded, he was well enough to be performing light duties in the wards. In the New Year he received the temporary rank of Major and was appointed Registrar at the Southall Hospital.

In late April 1917, after nine months in England, Claude reported for duty at the 2nd Australian General Hospital at Wimereux, south of Calais. Recently he must have received news of the death of his father, from heart disease at sixty-two, at his Aunt Mary's house in Neutral Bay. Soon after, from Cootamundra, his mother also moved to Neutral Bay, to 'Birkhall' in nearby Burroway Street. In June, at Wimereux, Claude's promotion was confirmed and on 6 September, at his own request, he was returned to the front.

In mid-September from the Belgian town of Wippenhoek, five miles west of Ypres, Major Tozer moved out with the 3rd Field Ambulance on rutted paths camouflaged with tattered hessian, past the ruins of Menin Gate and east towards Hooge. Claude's old Battalion, the Twelfth, was billeted nearby. So was Lieutenant Colonel Herbert St Vincent Welch, DSO and mentioned three times in despatches, now with the 13th Field Ambulance. Claude was assigned an advanced dressing station on the Menin Road near Hooge Tunnel. All around, the elaborate Belgian canal system had been destroyed by shelling, making the fields a quagmire of water and mud. Further east, beyond a string of forward clearing posts, lay the front lines. At dawn on 20 September, in heavy mist, the 12th Battalion left their dugouts with fixed bayonets to advance on Polygon Wood. In bitter cold, the first stretcher cases reached Claude at 9 a.m.

By nightfall it had rained heavily, and the remaining paths and duckboards were almost submerged. Claude, frustrated at constant backlogs and delays, sent a terse message back down the line to Lieutenant-Colonel Butler, his commanding officer, demanding more blankets and reinforcements. The incoming bearers must be *compelled* to carry equipment back to the collecting posts, he wrote; there was no other way to keep the front supplied. Then, with Menin Road impassable and the telephone line to the aid posts cut, he went forward alone to try to reorganise his teams.

Sometime in the same month Claude's name appeared in the records again when, somewhere behind the front lines, he was forced to amputate a corporal's leg without anaesthetic. By now he had had himself transferred back to the Twelfth, replacing their own badly wounded RMO. On 29 September Major General H.B. Walker, commander of the 1st Australian Division, wrote the recommendation for Claude's DSO.

'Not for myself,' Dorothy Mort would tell the chemist back in Sydney, with a hint of distracted, motherly worry. 'For my little boy. I've read in my medical book, a small amount mixed in warm olive oil, for earache? He cries so.' Each time, in a different place, Dorothy would say the same thing. Well-groomed, and with the authority of any respectable woman of good address, she would then put the small chemist's parcel in her bag, casually, and go back across the harbour and up the railway line to Lindfield.

In her bedroom in late 1920, in her silk kimono, Dorothy turned the key in the inside lock and placed the brown paper parcel in her drawer. There was little else to block the terrible thoughts that invaded her mind whenever she relaxed her guard.

As her children ran on the grass and played down by the bridge over the scrubby creek; as Miss Fizelle—hovering, anxious to please—sat on a cane chair with her mending, with her endless cups of milky tea on the little stone-pillared verandah; even as she sought to keep herself occupied with small domestic chores and caring for her children, she was tired.

She tried not to, but, again and again, she returned to the smallest drawer in the dressing table where she kept hidden the small brown bottle with its typed chemist's label.

※

In Flanders, as winter set in, wounded men and prisoners streamed past, moving back along a roadside littered with wrecked machinery and dead horses and mules, sometimes stopping to forage in the woods for a corpse's sodden greatcoat to use as a blanket. At the clearing stations the surgical teams of six worked constantly, four men on and two off, in shifts of sixteen hours.

All through the cold October of 1917, the concussed and shattered bodies flooded through the aid post. Any wound from the trenches—rat-infested, strewn with rusting wire, human excreta and putrefying body parts—was prone to infection. With an injury to the abdomen, when the cavity was fouled with faeces or intestinal matter, Claude knew, death was common. Chest wounds often recovered surprisingly well. Head injuries, unless the brain had suffered irretrievable insult, also did unexpectedly well. The skill lay in excising the wound and cutting away any damaged bone or pulped brain matter, and then (if it was readily locatable in the surface tissue with the tip of a finger), removing the projectile. Any temptation to probe more deeply was generally lethal. The wound would then be flushed with antiseptic Eusol, the scalp flaps sewn back together, and a drain inserted. If the wound began to heal within eight to ten days, the patient would survive. This, Claude noted with academic detachment, was approximately what had happened with himself.

In spite of his father's death, he had little time to mourn. He rode his bearers and orderlies hard, for efficiency's sake, and ultimately for their own good and safety. It was a strategy he knew was destined to make him more popular with his superiors than his subordinates.

On their brief leaves the enlisted men went to the town *estaminets*, looking for bad French beer and coarse cigarettes and milky coffee served in thick china bowls. At night, the back room door would often conceal a widow, or a good church-going daughter, who prayed that the War would end and the foreign soldiers would leave, but not before they had left their money behind. A story circulated of the ragged and starved magpie, tamed then abandoned by the retreating Germans, that arrived with querulous complaints in the English trenches. Superstitiously, the soldiers tried to keep it alive.

In his frontline dugout Claude hoarded his precious vials of morphine, firstly for painkilling, and then to calm the overwrought nerves of shell-shocked men whose screams and visions and inability to lie still was contagious, and could set off a chain reaction of hysteria that turned his aid post to chaos. He recognised the pallor and the fixed stare, the jerky mannerisms, the insensibility to the pricking of a pin or even a burning cigarette. Wherever they were, they could not be reached by any means he knew.

※

In Ralph Stock's novel *The Pyjama Man*, when Sprague's play fails in London, the playwright returns penniless to Sydney on a pre-war immigrant ship, but now, from his shabby theatrical boarding house near Wynyard station, the city seems wintry and unwelcoming. Then—in an unexpected denouement that takes place in the ballroom of the Kosciuszko Hotel—a friend arrives from New York to announce that the piece has been sold to Broadway for £400. Sprague and Meg are happily reunited, and marry.

The Pyjama Man, dedicated to 'friends in Manly', appeared with the NSW Bookstall Company in 1913. Norman Lindsay's colourful jacket this time showed a young man in pyjamas, smoking a pipe, on a beach with a dark-haired, barefoot girl wearing a swimsuit and kimono. On the back, an Orient Line advertisement lists fortnightly departures to England by the S.S. *Orontes, Orama, Orvieto, Otranto, Otway* and *Orsova*. But by this date, Stock was already back London.

The Pyjama Man by Ralph Stock, N.S.W. Bookstall Co, Sydney 1913. Cover by Norman Lindsay. Photo: by permission of the Lindsay Estate

By February 1914, however, he was in Sydney again, bringing his sister Mabel and a friend called Jackson with whom he planned to travel further in the Pacific. Pooling their money, they bought the *Wanderlust*, a 43-foot cedar yawl with a six horsepower engine and—it became evident soon after delivery—serious leaks. While expensive repairs were made at Rushcutters Bay, Stock hired a cine camera to practise film-making in the Botanical Gardens. By this time they had attracted the attention of the local press and, under such headlines as 'Lady's Venturesome Voyage', interviews with Mabel appeared in several newspapers.

In May the party set off and, after a problematic start, the *Wanderlust* was wrecked on arrival at Norfolk Island. Hitching a ride back to Sydney, the three bought commercial passages for Fiji, but were forced to return to Australia again when war was declared. In September Ralph and Mabel sailed for England, where Stock joined the Artists' Rifles, giving 'writer and author' as his occupation, 'nil' as his religion, and the Bank of New South Wales at Threadneedle Street in London as his address. On 12 April 1916—a week after Claude had embarked from Alexandria on the *Corsican* for Marseilles—2nd Lieutenant Ralph Stock was seconded to the Machine Gun Corps for active service in France.

In the last days of October 1917, as Claude convalesced from a bout of trench fever in hospital at Le Tréport on the wintry north-western French coast, someone in the hierarchy above him decided that he had had enough. In early December he was discharged from Le Tréport and assigned to the No. 3 Australian General Hospital at Abbeville, thirty miles downriver from Amiens. In the New Year, he received the news of his DSO.

On two weeks' leave in London before leaving for Abbeville, he drew his pay and a new uniform at the AIF office under the arches at 130 Horseferry Road. Soldiers strolled around Piccadilly, army overcoats belted against the cold, and surveyed the Tower, St Paul's Cathedral and Westminster Abbey: all those grey soot-stained edifices that the Australians often found disappointing compared to their expectations. In the dining room at the Dominion Forces Club near Vauxhall Bridge, the Australian Women's Reserve, in heavy woollen khaki, served them boiled mutton and onion sauce. At night the warden's lamps, painted blue, formed small pockets of light in the dimmed-out city.

In January 1918 the long straight road that led through bare French fields to the Abbeville hospital was glassy with ice. Inside the compound the snow piled knee-deep against the tented wards, so that even the fire buckets, positioned near the wood stoves that were supposed to warm the interiors, were frozen solid by morning.

A collection of wooden hutments smelling of creosote and newly-sawn timber, sufficient to shelter 2000 men, held patients in collapsible cots exactly two feet apart, each bound down tidily with grey blankets. In each bare corridor a straight-backed nurse in a red cape and elaborate veil kept guard at a small table. Claude worked in the acute surgical ward among the amputation and deep wounds cases, where the chill air reeked of Eusol with an underlying sickly-sweet note of gangrene. Here the patients were ranged three-deep in rows of ten, each with a drip vessel above his head.

By March the buildings had warmed a little and the tiny new saplings lining Howse Road were no longer buried deep in snow. Now the nurses brought in armfuls of blossom buds and greenery to place in the wards, and wildflowers appeared in jars in the officers' mess. Behind the Australian and South African Hospitals, slow-moving gangs of German prisoners laboured in the grounds.

On 23 June 1918, four months before the Armistice, Major Tozer and twenty-seven fellow officers lined up for a photograph in front of the Acute Surgical Ward. Once you have picked him out among the uniformed rows, your eyes tend to return to him. A well-made man, clean-cut, Claude sits squarely, his wide shoulders and straight back filling out the stiff dress tunic, his officer's cap sitting easily. While the men on either side look strained or severe, Claude's expression is almost resigned—the mouth set in an even line, the eyes creased down at the corners in what might be melancholy. His hands rest lightly on his jodhpured thighs and his feet in their polished boots and leggings are evenly placed. He looks older now than his twenty-eight years, and no longer affects the weedy moustache or the swagger stick of some of his fellows. Calm and dependable, he is the grown-up son that any Australian mother would be proud to call her own.

Major C. J. Tozer DSO in front of the Acute Surgical Ward at the 3rd Australian General Hospital, Abbeville, France, 23 June 1918. Photo: War Memorial EO2567

Some two weeks later, as poppies began to bloom amid the ripening wheat, Claude was returned to Headquarters at Horseferry Road in London. In September, after a further stretch at Abbeville, he was posted temporarily to Paris. The Germans sued for peace on the last day of the month, and the Armistice was signed on 11 November 1918. A week before Christmas, Claude embarked from Liverpool on the transport *Aeneas* for Sydney, arriving on 11 February 1919 after an absence of three and a half years.

Demobbed in early April, he re-joined his widowed mother Beatrice, who by now had left Birkhall in Neutral Bay for Shireen in Roseville. According to his medical records, Claude still complained of headaches and an inability to concentrate. Noted also was the bullet fragment lodged in his right temporal lobe, half an inch below the surface, and too close to the brain to be removed. Although his leg injury had healed, the severity of his head wound meant that he was classified as permanently unfit for further duty. Apart from that, his health was considered sound.

NINE

Manly in Winter

By July 1920, Claude had been home for just over eighteen months. Perhaps he was as moody and restless as many of the other returned men, as he struggled to establish his suburban medical practice and adjust to the confines of domestic life with his mother in Roseville. After three years of patching up badly-damaged soldiers only to send them back to their almost inevitable deaths in the trenches, something inside him must have seemed spent, even if the façade he presented to the world appeared intact. The warm admiration in the eyes of Dorothy Mort must have seemed a welcome distraction.

Despite their easy intimacy, Dorothy remained a creature of unpredictable moods and dark secrets. It was foreign territory to him, this female neurasthenia. Men suffered differently; even those with nerves shattered by shellshock. If, in studying the minute degrees between delusion, insanity and malingering, he had developed a sense for what is real and what is imaginary, he had had little opportunity for gaining an understanding of the female mind. Perhaps he sympathised at first with the earnest and well-meaning Harold, who—at the end of his tether, or his wits—absented himself at work or to his own interests, leaving his wife at home to brood on her malaises. All the same, Dorothy's fey manner and large, searching eyes were disquieting.

'I don't know why God made these neurotic women,' Claude told Beatrice Tozer soon after his first visit to Dorothy in May, as she tended to his appointment book. But by his second or third visit, still in the winter months of 1920, he had started to call her Diana, or Di—the name she affected for her stage appearances. This was not the name her husband used. In the straightforward company of soldiers, Claude had kept his emotions on a tight rein. Surely the time had come for a little light-heartedness?

Roseville,
Friday

Dearest Lady,

    There is one virtue I possess—there may be others which you and your sympathetic mind will reveal—and that virtue is never to break a promise, so here is the letter. To begin with, and to plagiarise the old Governor of North Carolina, 'it is a long time between meetings', but though the time drags slowly enough while waiting it seems to fly fast enough, and far too fast, when we do meet, which is funny, but true.

    The telepathic messages have been duly received, and if continued will no doubt make me a firm believer in Conan Doyle's spiritualistic theories. It is to be hoped that my messages as sent were received, and enabled you to get a little more sleep than usual—at any rate they were intended to comfort you, and in this way to help you through the dreary nights. It only shows how temperaments differ—the more anxious I am the better I sleep, although apparently my subconscious self is busy at work trying to unravel some problem, for in the morning a new aspect seems to dawn on me. So I think I must be, or have, a receptive soul—that is, if a doctor can have a soul; another little item for you to discover. There would certainly seem to be unfathomed depths in my make up which no one has yet troubled to explore, so there is an adventure for you. Try and worry out what is good in me, besides sympathy and reverence, and if you have done nothing else, you will then have something on the credit side when the Big Book is looked into at the end. Au revoir.

>   Yours longingly,
>   Claude
>   PS The road map is being obtained tomorrow.

Sir Arthur Conan Doyle had come to 'explore the unknown drama of the soul', he told the local press. A tall figure with a fine moustache and an attractive Scottish burr, in the late spring of 1920, lecturing on behalf of the British Psychical Research Society at the Sydney Town Hall, he had faced a crush of people cheering so loudly that it was a full ten minutes before they would let him speak. Many waved white handkerchiefs, a newspaper reported. Then someone in the crowd began to sing 'Lead, Kindly Light', and one after another, all over the room, everyone joined in.

'It is not altogether a sombre journey he makes among the shadows, but apparently one of happy, as well as tender experiences, so that laughter is not necessarily excluded from the exposition,' a journalist observed. The visitor also wanted to go among the Aborigines, believing that 'those who are close to nature might know something of its occult secrets'.

He had spoken for two hours—of his boy Kingsley, wounded on the Somme and then dead of pneumonia after the Great War, and of how he had been miraculously returned to him, the paper recorded. Through a medium in England, in a séance, he had actually talked with him—his own dead son! He even had a Spirit Photograph of him.

A man near the door had cried out 'Antichrist! Antichrist!', but soon was hushed and bundled out by those around him. Some other lone fanatic had cried out that it was the Devil who came to him, and not his son. But when the doctor affirmed so calmly, in his deep and kindly voice, that such a remark showed only the workings of a queer mind, what cheering erupted. Even Mr Hughes, the prime minister, wanted to meet him.

As he passed out of the hall, they had crowded around him, close enough to touch, murmuring 'God bless you'. Even to the door of Petty's Hotel, where he had left his wife and children, they had gathered about him. Now he was to visit Manly, for the surf bathing. A steamer trip from the pier, and a picnic, had been organised by the Sydney spiritualists who had invited him there.

But was it always a good thing, Dorothy might have wondered, to talk with the dead?

Mrs Mort's Madness

Shireen,
Boundary Street,
Roseville
16/8/20

Dearest Lady,

      I have not written during the weekend, not having the opportunity and not being in the mood, owing to worry over a seriously ill case; and even this hurried note is to say I can't get around this week, partly due to professional duties; but more so due to business reasons connected with the mater and myself. I have to visit town to see the War Service Homes people, and then a solicitor is coming out to see me on Wednesday. The best thing is to give me your Manly address, and I can write you there—

      Yours sorrowfully,
      Claude

TEN

Interlude

Roseville,
Friday

Dearest Little Lady,

    I am in serious mood tonight, probably because lack of patients has given me plenty of time to think. Naturally the thoughts are of you—there is nothing else now to be interested in, except work, to conquer the hunger, but—and it is a such a big but—where is it all going to lead us, and when or how is it going to finish? It is, really, a very apparent problem, because it always brings you up against the same old problem of—nowhere. And then you try to think around the stone wall and see if there is any way of overcoming it, and I cannot see one, so the only thing to do is to gather happiness while we may and let things slide, which is admittedly dangerous, and, at the same time, not very satisfying. You know—or you should know by now, Di—that I am never happier than when you are near me. Even the sight of you seems to comfort me, which is all very well for the present, but that platonic kind of existence cannot go on forever. I have never believed in it. And there is the future, because as sure as the sun rises and sets, one day I will forget, and then there is nothing between us and damnation except your purity and strength. Don't blame me too much, Di, if my reserve goes to the winds some day. There is in every one of us some deep-seated fountain of emotion—call it passion if you like. Mine has never been tapped, except by you, and some day the pressure will be too great for me, and who knows what I would say or do? You have stirred me to such an extent, little lady, that you are now sitting metaphorically on a sleeping volcano. I am pretty restrained, I know, because I have tried to be for years, but for you that restraint is very nearly gone. I can't explain why. There is hardly one woman who has ever attracted me before, but they say you get it badly when you fall, and there is no explanation. So, lady fair, it is better to take stock of things now, before I break out, and consider what is to be done. At present I am content to glide on the river of bliss, but the small conscience sits on the bank, and shows the danger signal. Still, *nous verrons*, for the moment, everything is nothing, except another day gone, and Tuesday is nearer.

> *Tout mon amour,*
> Claude

By this stage there is no going back. No one knows how it played out, but one can imagine.

On one of these morning visits, in the sanctioned intimacy of his profession, he finds himself sitting closer to her than he should, as he lies propped on her pillows. Almost without knowing it, he reaches out and his fingers brush her cheek. They both know immediately that this brief contact is different from the routine touch of his stethoscope below her collarbone, his eyes focused on the middle distance, or as he taps to test the soundness of her lungs, or measures her pulse with his fingers on her thin wrist as merely a diagnostic tool.

This first time, perhaps, he draws back. Next time they meet, he thinks, they will mutely—tacitly—be in accord that it did not happen. Nothing has changed. But already he is measuring the hours until he can decently return.

It isn't as if, in recent months, he hasn't met suitable young women: they come readily to watch him play on field and court and openly try to catch his eye. All those respectable North Shore doctors' and clergymen's daughters, living at home, sheltered by their families; young girls who, if even slightly compromised, must eventually be married. But compared to her, no doubt, they seem callow and uninteresting.

Claude, stirred by unrecognised physical anticipation, is gripped by a hunger that his rational mind cannot subdue. At her bedside, he stares at her uncomprehendingly, torn by an internal conflict. She gazes back, not moving. He cannot know what she is thinking, but there is no nervousness, no embarrassment, in her gaze.

His forefinger slides beneath the cuff of her white nightgown, with its insets of fine lace, and he strokes the blue veins inside her wrist. At first she does not respond, as his mouth brushed hers with a sensation like electricity. Then her eyelids close, slowly. As his mouth moves gently over her face, and back to her lips, he hears her almost silent sigh, even as he wills himself to turn back, to stand up, to turn away.

This is not what he intended.

But then his hands slide down from her shoulders and meet around her thin spine and draw her to him. She shifts a little so that her slight body is within his arms. He feels the fine bones of her ribs almost frangible under his fingers, through the thin white lace, and his hand moves, unbidden, to cup her small breast in his palm through the translucent cloth. As if in a dream, he fumbles at the tiny pearl buttons of her nightdress; he cannot prevent his hands from following an age-old convoluted path of clumsy unfastenings and entrapping fabric as, inch by inch, he lays bare her pale skin to the cool electric air. After what seemed an age, they are at last both unencumbered, and he pushes back the tangled covers and matches himself to her, lips to lips, breast to breast, belly to belly, until even their bare feet seek each other out.

In her nest of tumbled linen she moves, as if instinctively, to fit herself more closely to him. When he can bear it no longer, the awful exhilaration, in some bright-lit garden of Eden made dazzling by his own long sexual frustration, he becomes aware of her hands on his back, drawing him to her ever more perfectly.

It ends quickly this time; and yet still they cling to each other, closing out the world beyond them. Wanting the moment to last forever.

It might have been hard for Claude, back in his university days, to imagine just how the sort of respectable women he knew—the decent, virginal sisters of his school friends; the light-hearted, flirtatious girls who danced with him at College balls under crepe paper streamers and pictures of the King—could become the passionate sexual counterparts he had read about in books. How did an everyday situation—indeed, any social encounter with a young woman—translate itself into an amorous occasion? How did these passions take over? And now, with every nerve-ending laid bare, he knew.

'I will make you care for me as I care for you,' he told her. And meant it.

As the days and months went by, and Claude was drawn in more deeply into Dorothy's world, he might not immediately have recognised the gravity of her periods of melancholy, and what they might portend. His own unhappiness, when it occurred, was firmly based in the real—the experience of war, of friends lost, of suffering. He did not recognise the danger in her near-panic when he did not visit her; the despair at even his short absences; the sort of panic that sent her to her bed and made her useless to her children, unable to fulfil even the simplest household task. Her illness was a thing built in her own interior consciousness, not rooted in the outside world, and therefore, to him, perhaps not entirely real. Nevertheless, he perceived something fine and good in her.

She needed distraction, to be brought out of herself, to be grounded in the real world, he probably thought. And something to help her sleep at night, so that her debilitated mind was not subject to such phantasms.

Mrs Mort's Madness

On 3 December 1920, sweltering under an overcast sky at the Woolloongabba in Brisbane, Claude stood poised for flight. A preparatory match against the visiting English Marylebone Cricket Club in front of a crowd of around 4000, he waited for the big Yorkshireman Waddington to bowl the opening ball to Herbie Collins. This was the most important game of his career. On the tropical green his white ducks were already sweat-sodden, his sleeves rolled tight above the elbow, the wide-brimmed sun hat taut across his forehead.

And perhaps it was now, away in Queensland, that he recognised the precipice before him. With 500 miles between them, he could visualise a life without Dorothy Mort. Now he saw her clearly, wan and pale in her dim and lifeless house in Lindfield, waiting only for him. Was it suddenly suffocating, the vision? There was no doubt of the depth of her feeling. But what had begun innocently had gone too far, and threatened to destroy them both.

He would end it. Finally. On his return.

The crack of leather on willow sounded at the other end of the pitch. Claude ran.

ELEVEN

To the City

In early December 1920, a few days before the rain, Dorothy smoothed her long white dress, pulled her hat low over her face, and went out the garden gate. White stockings and summer shoes, daytime white kid gloves: her outward appearance was impeccable. As she walked along the unpaved footpath, past the line of neat wooden fences towards the station, she might have thought about turning back. At the height of summer the sun had wilted the hydrangeas and sucked the humidity from the grass, and ahead lay the hour-long journey on the rattling train to Milsons Point, where the bustle and noise of horses and motor cars at the punt ferry met the glitter of the harbour. But the imperative was too great. It had to be to the city this time. To frequent the same place twice on the same errand would risk being remembered, even questioned. She couldn't tell the same story again at Sinclair's in Lindfield. Any reputable pharmacist would recognise her reasons immediately. So she made her way to the station, over the railway bridge where the horse-drawn cabs waited idly for fares, and onto the platform.

Mrs Mort's Madness

Another day in early December. Dorothy had first noticed the two men on New South Head Road. They had stayed on the tram with her all the way to Rose Bay. She was sure they were watching her, but always their glances seemed to slide away whenever she raised her head. She knew they would get down at the same stop. Even without turning her head she could feel their eyes upon her.

Inside the gates of 'Ellerslie', the big house in Rose Bay that the producer Arthur Shirley had made his temporary studio, was a stone bench. It was here that they would wait for her, pretending to be in idle conversation, just as they'd done on the tram. But even as she turned to point them out, they were gone. She was certain they were there, she told him.

Mr Shirley turned to look at the bench. 'But there is no one there,' he said.

On 15 December 1920, in the late afternoon at Circular Quay, Dorothy crossed the tram tracks and passed under the stone portals of the Customs House. From there she slipped into the shadow of the old Mort & Co. building, before entering the slow rise of Loftus Street. At Macquarie Place, chained off behind iron bollards and a dozen feet above the pavement, the tall, narrow bronze personage of Thomas Sutcliffe Mort gazed down at her from his rococo pedestal, right hand resting authoritatively on his hip, left leg still striding towards a promising future.

Thomas Sutcliffe Mort at Macquarie Place. Photo: unknown

At Castlereagh Street, among the cluster of pawnbrokers and second-hand jewellers between King and Park Streets, she hesitated outside No. 77. Thick glass, an iron mesh grill, the name Mont de Piété in tarnished gilt. A bell clanged as she pushed it open; a man emerged from behind a partition. She had rehearsed what she would say. Surely many respectable married women came here to sell an item of jewellery no longer worn?

'It's rather old fashioned,' she told him. 'I have no further use for it.'

From behind the counter, William John Beattie sized up her tasteful outfit, the single string of good pearls, the plain gold wedding band, the modulated voice.

'Of course,' he said. 'A fine piece. Five pounds.'

The woman in white looked up, startled. 'But surely ... I had it valued at Fairfax and Roberts. Ten pounds at least, it was said.'

Beattie shrugged and slid the brooch back across the counter. The woman paused, then pushed it forward again. Beattie filled out the receipt. She took the single note without looking up, and left. When Beattie looked down at the docket he saw that the name she had signed was Diana Reay.

❧

Several blocks away on King Street, Dorothy entered another shop, again a well-dressed housewife on an ordinary errand. Again she had practised in front of the glass, making her gestures and expressions appropriate to that rarity: a woman shopping innocently for a gun.

'A present for a man who is going abroad, to Morocco,' she said. 'Ralph Stock, the famous author, do you know of him? He was in the newspapers, only just recently. My husband is travelling with him at present.'

The pistol was small and smooth and squat, made of a dull, creamy blue-grey metal, and surprisingly heavy.

'And how does it work?' she asked, opening wide her eyes with womanly curiosity.

William Cowles, the gunsmith, slipped the magazine deftly from the butt and pressed the small nickel demonstration cartridges into it one after the other; and then, with quick fingers, clicked on and off the safety mechanism and demonstrated the cocking movement.

'A gift for my husband, going to India,' Dorothy murmured again, as he wrapped the oiled cardboard box in brown paper, tied it with string, and slid it across the counter. But had she contradicted herself, she wondered as she left the shop. Had she not first said Morocco?

TWELVE

Ingelbrae, Tuesday, 21 December 1920

'Come into the drawing room with me,' Dorothy said as he sat down at her bedside and Miss Fizelle turned away and closed the door. 'I have something to give you. Just a little thing. A memento.'

Claude followed her obediently, looking drawn and pale. As he sat on the Chesterfield settee writing out her prescription, Dorothy took the tiny package from a drawer at the back of the room. She leant over him from behind, her hand on his shoulder, while he carefully undid the string. She had almost lost the moment, in delaying too long; in a few seconds, cradling the locket in the palm of his hand, he would turn to thank her. His eyes would seek out hers, expecting to find love and trust. She could not bear that. She brought her other hand quickly from behind her back as he slowly started to turn towards to her, as if in surprise.

Hours later, Dorothy lay against Claude's chest as

though she were in a dream. She had done up his waistcoat and slipped her hand beneath his jacket, but now there was no heartbeat, even though he was still warm. Lifting his arm she placed it comfortingly around her shoulders, and took his hand in hers. He did not draw her close, as he always did, but neither did he move away. She waited for the medicine to take effect, and soon the ache in her left side was reduced to a dull throb. She had no idea how long she had been here like this; but it seemed like a long time. Now everything would be all right. He would not leave her, and they would never have to worry about anything again. As she lay safe in his arms, waiting for sleep to come, she heard a tapping outside. Was it Florence, knocking tentatively on the door yet?

'Everything's all right,' she called out.

When she woke again, she was still lying against Claude's chest. She tried to lift his wrist to look at his watch, and realised it was late afternoon, and his hand was cold. His arm was stiff; his embrace imprisoning rather than comforting.

The tapping outside continued and, at last, with time passing, she recognised it for what it surely was: her husband carpentering her coffin. She closed her eyes and waited for him to finish.

Part Two

The Investigation and the Trial

THIRTEEN

Claude at Rest

Looking today at the black and white police photograph printed in *Truth* on 20 March 1921, between the coroner's inquest and the trial, it is not immediately apparent that the man on the chesterfield settee is dead. The picture lacks the filtered romanticism generally associated with period photographs, despite a composition so symmetrical it could be a stage set. The room is sparsely furnished. Claude Tozer, at the centre of the viewfinder, is lying back with his legs outstretched, a lone diagonal in a field of verticals, framed on either side by two straight wooden chairs. His large, strong hands rest lightly on his trousered thighs, his fingers curled slightly as if in repose. His shirt cuffs do not show below his jacket sleeves, which have been pulled up quite high on his wrists. His eyes are closed. It is a peaceful picture. Apart from the bloodstains on the sofa, the only item out of place is the occasional table—a large oval Benares brass tray—that has been laid to one side with its ornately-carved collapsible wooden legs on top. The leather soles of Claude's new black shoes are pristine.

Suzanne Falkiner

A crime scene photograph inscribed 'Dr Tozer Murder' was published unmodified in the *Sun*, 20 March 1921, and in the *Daily Telegraph*. Photo: NSW Police Forensic Photography Archive, Justice and Police Museum, Historic Houses Trust of NSW

These days, we expect newspaper photographs of the dead to be safely distanced—by the military uniforms of some foreign country, or with faces deliberately obscured, or by the bodies being positioned just far enough from the lens for death's more banal details to be beyond our notice. Anonymously archival, or made safely portentous by an historical past. We do not expect to see someone who might be our neighbour lying dead as we drink our morning cup of tea.

FOURTEEN

Miss Fizelle's Nightmare of a Day

> Ever since the shooting occurred the house has been besieged by a young army of eager detectives. Papers were overhauled, and photographs and other things carefully scrutinised, and the assistance of fingerprint experts secured. Perhaps the most important finds ... were some letters, the blood-stained pieces of a photograph which had been torn up, and an unfinished prescription in the doctor's handwriting ... there was some writing on the back [of the photograph] which the police took to be [that] of Dr Tozer.
>
> —*Truth*, Sunday, 26 December 1920

According to the morning papers of Wednesday 22 December 1920, the day after the events, the 'Lindfield tragedy' was the main topic of conversation in the city. Detective Inspector Arthur Leary, the officer in charge of the investigation, was forthcoming with the journalists who besieged the house, even allowing them inside to view the body.

At forty-seven, sallow-complexioned and solidly built, Leary had been a policeman for twenty years, and a detective with the Metropolitan Criminal

Investigation Department for ten of them. An Irish Catholic from a rural family from Bombala, the previous year he and two associates had been summonsed to answer an accusation of assaulting a suspect, although in the event the complainant had declined to press the charge. More than once the unusual expansiveness of the confession a criminal had felt impelled to make to him had found unfavourable attention in court. During the famous IWW—or Wobblies—inquiry of 1918, Leary had been obliged to defend a fellow officer, Detective Sergeant Stewart Robson, from a claim that he had loaded up an arson suspect with an incendiary device—although, as Leary maintained, Robson couldn't have done it, as they had searched the man's bag together, and he would have noticed. Neither had an allegation of bribery stuck. A methodical man, Leary had been already twice commended for the thoroughness of his work, and his promotion through the ranks had been regular. The Mort case made a change from the usual lowlife murders, assaults and robberies that came his way.

Florence Fizelle—whose name the newspapers initially took down as 'Miss Frances Fraser'—had told police that Dr Tozer had arrived at Ingelbrae to see Mrs Mort at about 11 a.m. Around noon, reported the *Sydney Morning Herald*, she had heard a noise and gone to the room the two were in, only to hear Mrs Mort say from inside that 'everything was all right'. Later, becoming suspicious, she had tried to telephone Mr Mort in Sydney from a neighbour's, but failed to do so. When, 'sometime after lunch', her room was broken into, Mrs Mort was found lying unconscious with a bullet wound to her left breast.

Wednesday afternoon's *Sun* recorded that Miss Fizelle, after trying a number of times to telephone a doctor from the neighbour's, had returned to the house to find Mrs Mort's little daughter there, and the two of them together had knocked at the locked drawing room door without success. The bedroom door, which had been open when Miss Fizelle went to telephone, was now also closed and locked. Although they had banged on it repeatedly through the afternoon, it remained shut fast and, from within, Mrs Mort continued to tell them that nothing was wrong.

'The Tozer Tragedy': Ingelbrae 'Mr H.S. Mort's residence at Lindfield, where the tragedy occurred.' Image: *Truth* Sunday 20 March 1921, page 7

On Thursday the *Herald* picked up the threads again. Dr Tozer had been in the drawing room with Mrs

Mort for a considerable amount of time, police had revealed. The paper also quoted Miss Fizelle—now described as a 'lady companion'—as saying that, after hearing what might have been shots, she had tried to call a doctor but had found the neighbour's telephone 'out of order'. On her return Mrs Mort had again assured her that nothing was wrong, but at seven that evening when she finally pushed her way into the bedroom it was to find her mistress 'covered with blood and in a state of collapse'. Friends who had come to the house then communicated with the police.

Thursday's *Daily Telegraph* elaborated that Miss Fizelle, having shown Dr Tozer to his patient's bedroom and closed the door, had gone to the back of the house. A few minutes later, hearing what she took to be shots—she did not know how many—from the drawing room, she had gone running to the door and found it locked.

'It struck me as strange that apparently Dr Tozer and Mrs Mort were in the drawing room, because I did not think that Mrs Mort was able to get out of bed, she was so ill,' Miss Fizelle told the journalist. 'I was not satisfied, so I went to a neighbour's place to ring up.' Later, finding the doors to both rooms locked, she had several times brought iced water at Mrs Mort's request and left it outside the bedroom. At seven in the evening, she had finally gained entrance. 'At this point of the story,' reported the *Sun*, 'Miss Fraser [Fizelle] broke off. She said that she could hardly remember anything more, she was so upset.'

On Sunday 26 December, the day after Christmas, the weekly scandal sheet *Truth*, owned by young Ezra Norton, entered the fray with an overview of the events. What took place after Harold Mort had summoned Dr Tozer to Mrs Mort's bedside nobody knew, the paper commented; not even the 'lady help' who was in the house the whole time. Unless Mrs Mort recovered sufficiently to fill in the blanks, the matter might never be cleared up.

According to *Truth*, the police report to the Coroner held that Dr Tozer's visit—'allegedly professional'—to Mrs Mort's bedside had begun at about 11.30 a.m., and continued in the drawing room. 'Eventually Mrs Mort must have crossed the hallway and entered her own bedroom unnoticed, as about 5 p.m. she called from there for a drink of "ice cold water". She repeated the order soon after as she "was terribly thirsty". The help was not allowed to enter the room, but had to leave the water on each demand at the door, when it would be surreptitiously taken by Mrs Mort.' Later Miss Fizelle had helped her mistress to bed. *Truth* concluded that until the Coroner's own report was handed down at the inquest, little more could be established.

This took place nearly three months later, on 14 March 1921, when Miss Fizelle's account was further refined and amplified. Mrs Mort had been ill in bed and in very low spirits when Dr Tozer arrived, according to Florence. Ten minutes later, from the back of the house, she had heard what she took to be a shot, but was not entirely sure. Finding Mrs Mort's bedroom empty and the door ajar, she had tried the drawing room door, directly opposite, only to find that it was locked, and Mrs Mort, from inside, had refused to admit her.

'I then went and telephoned a message for Mr Mort to come home as soon as he could. I went to the back of the house and heard two more shots,' said Miss Fizelle. This was roughly about ten minutes after the first shot, reported the *Sydney Morning Herald*—or, according to the *Telegraph*, 'between ten and twenty minutes.' The second and third shots, Florence thought, were 'almost together'.

Florence herself had then fainted dead away for several hours, she maintained. Coming to 'a long time afterward', she found herself lying on the verandah. 'Some time afterwards the children asked me where their mother was. One of them went to the locked door and called out to their mother, who answered that everything was all right.'

Miss Fizelle had tried the drawing room door again herself between 3 and 4 p.m., when Mrs Mort, from inside, had asked for iced water, while repeating that she was 'quite all right'. Florence took the water to the locked door and left it there. Dr Tozer's car, she saw, was still outside. Then she went out on the grass with the children until about 5 p.m., when she found that the door to the bedroom was also now locked, with Mrs Mort inside.

'I gave the children their tea, and put them to bed. That was about 7 p.m.,' Florence said. 'Again I went to Mrs Mort's door and asked her to let me in.' Again Mrs Mort refused, and again asked for iced water. 'I brought it. I heard her trying to open the door, and after some time she got it open. I returned, and she tried to shut the door, but I pushed my way in.

'Mrs Mort had a skirt on over her nightdress. I tried to do something for her, but she would not let me. Eventually I assisted her with hot water, and got her to bed.'

From this point on, it seemed, everything continued to happen with agonising slowness. After putting Dorothy to bed, Florence again went next door to Mr Wallace, the owner of the telephone, and asked him to call a doctor. William Smaillie, an architect living in nearby Russell Avenue was also alerted, and together with another neighbour, George Kenworthy from Tryon Road, he and his wife went to Ingelbrae at about 8.30 p.m., where they found Mrs Mort unconscious in her bed. A doctor had still not materialised, and so Messrs Smaillie and Kenworthy went to summon Dr James Murray, also of Tryon Road. Dr Murray accompanied them back to Ingelbrae—but still no one called the police.

On arriving at the house at about 9 p.m. on 21 December, Dr Murray would testify, he found Mrs Mort—whom he had never attended before—lying on her back in bed, wearing a nightdress and covered by bedclothes. She appeared deeply asleep and partially comatose; pale and breathing heavily through her mouth, and although she was muttering to herself, he couldn't understand her. Nor could he rouse her sufficiently to answer his questions.

Examining her further, he discovered a bullet wound—about the size of a three-penny bit—near her left breast, and a similar bullet hole close to the shoulder blade. She had blood on her body from her breast to her ankles, but at this early stage Murray was unsure whether the bullet had entered from the front or the back. He also noticed her parched tongue and, on opening her eyelids, her contracted pupils. At around this point, sometime after nine, the neighbour William Smaillie had telephoned Pymble police station.

On receiving Smaillie's call, the sergeant-in-charge at Pymble had sent two plainclothes constables to the house and telephoned Inspector Souter, his superior at North Sydney District. Souter in turn had alerted the City police. Constable Alfred Marden, from Pymble, had arrived at Ingelbrae soon after 9.30 p.m., he testified, where Florence Fizelle met him and handed him two keys, asking him to open the dining room door.

'Something has happened here,' she told him.

Marden had noted the house's layout: a short passage from the front door, with several small bedrooms to the left, and the larger conjoined dining and drawing rooms, each with its separate door to the hall, on the right. The kitchen was at the back, and Miss Fizelle's room behind that. Marden had opened the dining room door as requested and, over the partition, saw Dr Tozer's body in the drawing room. After discovering his bullet wounds, he also observed that the drawing room door was locked from the inside, with the key still in it, while the windows, too, were securely fastened from inside. He noticed what he described as a 'Colt revolver' near the body, and several empty cartridge shells scattered about. At that point, he also rang the City Police. Superintendents J.I. Bannan and C. Nolan, along with two detectives, Leary and Ramsay, set out by car from the Metropolitan Police Centre, at the corner of Phillip and Hunter Streets, at 10 p.m.

Meanwhile, at Ingelbrae, Mrs Mort's various other symptoms—most notably her dry tongue and contracted pupils—had caused Dr Murray to suspect she had been poisoned, probably by some narcotic. He had looked around for prescriptions or medicine bottles, but found nothing. When he finished his search he noticed her breathing and colour had become much worse, and the muttering had ceased. Dr Murray returned to his house for a rubber tube to pump her stomach.

Meanwhile, two plainclothes constables from North Sydney station had also arrived, and the bedroom was a hive of activity. On Mrs Mort's dressing table Marden found, among other things, another key to the dining room door, and—in a drawer—a letter signed 'Claude'. On his return Dr Murray, with the help of police, washed out Mrs Mort's stomach and gave her a hypodermic antidote.

The City police arrived about 11 p.m. Harold Mort had also arrived home at around 10.30 p.m., unaware of all these events, to be greeted by Dr Murray at the door. He had spent Tuesday afternoon with relatives in the eastern suburbs, he told the detectives, and had reached Circular Quay shortly after nine o'clock. Miss Fizelle confirmed that Mr Mort had told her he would be late, as he had business at Botany, and had said not to keep dinner for him.

On first seeing the body at Ingelbrae that night, Detective Inspector Leary testified later, he had observed a large pool of blood on the sofa on Dr Tozer's right side, and a bloodstained kimono partly underneath his right arm. In a wastepaper basket about eight feet away he had found a photograph of

Mrs Mort and Dr Tozer's visiting card, both torn up and bloodstained. On the drawing room floor was an empty bottle, which, when he sniffed it, led him to suspect it had contained laudanum, a preparation of opium. At this, Dr Murray washed out Mrs Mort's stomach several more times. The bottle, along with Mrs Mort's stomach contents, were put aside to be sent to Dr Cooksey, the Government Analyst. By this point Dorothy's pulse had improved, and a nurse had arrived and so, feeling less anxious about her, at about 1.30 a.m. Dr Murray went home.

On the same night, Leary later told the criminal court, he had interviewed Florence Fizelle and spoken to Harold Mort, who said that his wife had been ill for about seven months. When Leary had asked him if he had noticed anything wrong with her mentally, Mr Mort had replied, 'No, nothing at all'. When he inquired if he had known that Mrs Mort and Dr Tozer were on intimate terms, Harold had refused to discuss the matter.

Constable Marden again searched Mrs Mort's bedroom. Hidden under several hats on a wardrobe shelf he discovered two cardboard boxes for .32 calibre Colt automatic pistols. Inside one of these was a smaller box of thirty-six live nickel bullets, similar to the empty cartridges he had picked up in the drawing room. Harold Mort stated that he did not own a pistol and had seen neither weapon nor cartridges before. At about 5 a.m. Marden, in the bedroom, found three more letters from Claude to Dorothy.

With Mrs Mort too ill to speak, Police Superintendent Bannan from the City decided to leave the rest of the enquiry until morning. Officers were placed in charge of the scene, and Dr Tozer's body was left where it was.

FIFTEEN

The Investigation

On Wednesday morning, 22 December 1920, reported a newspaper, thirteen officers from three police stations were at the house. These included Constable Marden and two more men from Pymble; Superintendent Bannan and Detectives Leary, Anderson, Sedgwick, Wickham and Ramsay from the City; and the two constables from North Sydney. Two more officers, Sergeant Ferguson and Constable Howard, were making sketches and taking photographs.

Little had been disturbed overnight, and Ingelbrae was calm and peaceful, the *Sun* recorded that afternoon. Dr Murray had arrived again at 7 a.m. and was in close attendance. Dr Tozer's body, in a seemingly natural position, still lay on the chesterfield settee in the drawing room. On top of his thigh, near his open right hand, was a light Colt automatic pistol with several live cartridges still in the magazine. Three ejected cartridge shells had been recovered from the sofa and two from the floor nearby. Two bullet holes had been found in the back of the sofa and the wall, and another spent bullet was found lodged in a dining room chair.

There was no sign of a struggle. Lying at Claude's right side, Mrs Mort's blood-stained kimono also had a bullet hole in it. There was blood on the sofa, the carpet, and on several articles of furniture. A glass tumbler sat on the floor. Under the sofa, along with a partly-smoked cigarette, police found an unfinished medical prescription, which the doctor was believed to have been writing 'at the moment of the tragedy'. The three letters from Claude that Constable Marden had found in Mrs Mort's bedroom were written in 'calm' tones, according to the *Sun*. Being naturally very upset, Mr Mort had declined to speak to the press.

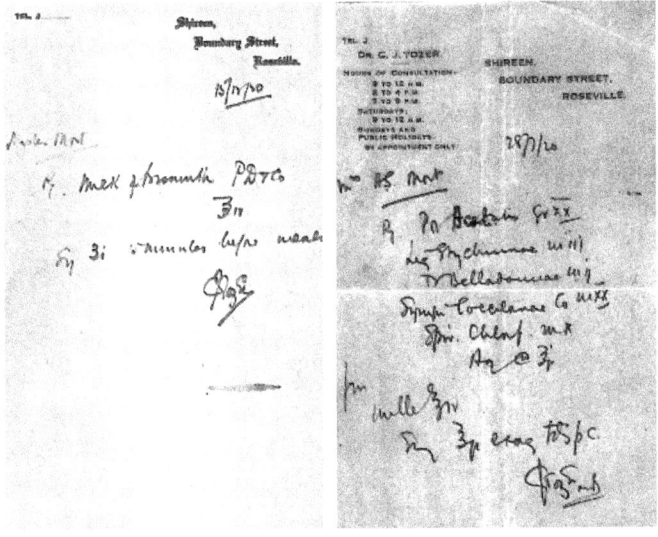

Above and following page: Dr Tozer's prescriptions, offered as evidence at Mrs Mort's trial. Photo: NSW Government Archives

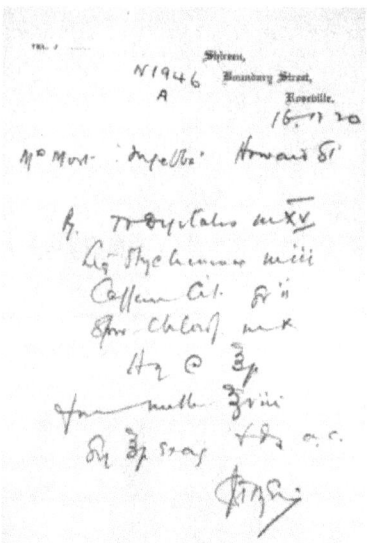

At 7 a.m. Dr Murray had found his patient conscious but drowsy. Mrs Mort was reported to be semi-conscious for most of the day, and talking a good deal in her delirium. At four in the afternoon, when Murray visited her again, she was fully conscious and much improved physically, but still very weak. Nevertheless, Dr Murray steadfastly refused to allow detectives to question her. His patient was at present unfit to make a statement, he told police, and any undue excitement could have serious consequences. However, both police and journalists had interviewed a 'highly excited' Miss Fizelle. By the afternoon the Government Medical Officer Arthur Palmer had viewed Dr Tozer's body *in situ*, and it was taken to the morgue.

The City Coroner's Court and Morgue, built on the site of the old 'dead house' of convict days at 104 George Street in the Rocks, was a dark brick Federation-style structure with an elegant columned arcade overlooking Circular Quay. Inside, dim corridors led to cool shady rooms equipped with marble slabs and all the arcane tools—scalpels, kidney dishes, metal rulers, rods and callipers, and the various saws, small and larger—needed for dissection.

At 3.30 p.m. Palmer and his colleague Dr Stratford Sheldon performed a post-mortem, witnessed by Robert Lee-Brown, the Medical Officer at Long Bay Penitentiary; and a Dr McKay. After the chest and stomach had been opened and examined, Dr Sheldon had peeled back the scalp, took a saw to the skull, and lifted out Dr Tozer's brain. When his observations were complete, the body was removed to Wood, Coffill and Co's funeral parlour near Central Station.

Although Detective Inspector Leary still refused to publicly identify the victim and perpetrator, another officer had revealed to the newspapers that—to them at least—the shooting was no longer a mystery.

'Who Fired the Shots?' demanded the *Sun* in a large headline the same afternoon.

The following morning, Thursday, Dr Murray finally permitted Detective Inspector Leary to speak to Dorothy Mort in her bedroom, and she told him she didn't wish to make a statement. When asked if anyone had instructed her not to do so, she answered, 'No', but allowed him search the room in her presence.

'In a dressing table drawer I found a small heart-shaped locket with a ribbon attached,' Leary testified later. 'Inside it was some hair and a small piece of paper with the words written on it: "Should anything happen to me, please bury this with me. DM".'

While he was looking around in the bedroom, Leary went on, Mrs Mort asked him if the police had found two letters of hers, one to Mrs Tozer and another to her mother in New Zealand. When Leary said he believed the police did have some letters of hers, she said, 'Well, tell them not to post them.' Soon after this he had found the two letters in question, stamped but unposted.

That afternoon, escorted by a female special constable, Dorothy was taken by ambulance to the Royal North Shore Hospital at St Leonards, from where the medical superintendent, Dr Emma Buckley, announced that she could not be moved again until her condition improved. Although said to be to be progressing favourably—she was now quite rational, not much perturbed by the events, and quite willing to make a statement to the police at her bedside, revealed the newspapers—she would not do so until the doctors pronounced her capable.

On the same day, Claude's two clergyman uncles, Reverend Leopold Charlton and Canon William Apedaile Charlton, conducted his funeral at Wood Coffill's Mortuary Chapel at 810 George Street. Four more of his Charlton uncles attended, including Percie the cricketer, along with numerous Charlton cousins and a large contingent of cricket officials and players, medical associates and members of the Roseville Tennis Club. No Morts or Tozers were noted among the mourners listed in Friday's *Herald*, nor the names of any women.

The Reverend Leopold Charlton.
Photo: Unknown

'Sterling worth which commands such respect must surely be the finest thing in one's character, and it is on character we must be judged,' pronounced the Reverend Leopold Charlton at the graveside at Waverley Cemetery. The presence of so many bespake of something sterling in Claude's character, Leopold went on, and it would be a great relief to his mother to know of their tribute in her hour of sorrow.

In the meantime, detectives, photographers and fingerprint experts had gathered again at Ingelbrae, searching for further clues, and the police disclosed that Dr Tozer had *not* fired the shots. There was little more for the journalists to go on, reported the *Herald*: all hinged now on what Mrs Mort would have to say at the coroner's inquiry, which would not be held until she was well enough to go into the witness box.

Oddly, however, what few knew (or perhaps chose to reveal), was that on Wednesday, the day after Claude's death, Dorothy had asked for Beatrice Tozer to visit her bedside at Ingelbrae and—even more oddly—the two women had been permitted to talk privately for some time.

Christmas came and went, and the *Telegraph* briefly observed that Dorothy's condition remained serious, while the *Herald* dropped the story entirely. On Sunday 26 December *Truth* revealed that the bottle found by police in the drawing room had contained laudanum: 'a discovery to which they attached no little importance'. This fact, coupled with Dr Murray's opinion that Mrs Mort had suffered some form of poisoning, gave them 'no small amount of mental exercise'.

Then the scandal rag dropped a bombshell.

Seven years ago, it appeared, Dorothy's father William Mackay Woodruff, an otherwise well-respected businessman and loving husband, had tried to kill his wife and son and then himself. While the lives of all three had hung by a thread for days, all had eventually recovered. With no apparent motive, and Woodruff himself proven to be unquestionably insane, the paper reported, no criminal proceedings had followed.

Mrs Mort's Madness

A more assiduous check of the dailies in mid-November 1913, however, might have revealed that Mackay Woodruff had indeed been charged and imprisoned. The incident had first come to light at about 5.15 a.m. on Monday 22 September that year, when a Dr James Isbister, of Miller Street in North Sydney, received an almost incoherent telephone call from Mackay's son Ronald Woodruff.

'Something dreadful has happened,' Ronald told him.

When Dr Isbister had arrived at 'Kyellah' in Crows Nest Road, Ronald had staggered to the door to meet him with bloodied hands pressed to his forehead and in a state of near-collapse. Isbister had called immediately for an ambulance and the police.

Ronald revealed later that his mother and father had spent the weekend at Leura in the Blue Mountains, and he had gone to meet their train at about nine-thirty on the Sunday night. He had accompanied them home, and all were asleep in their separate bedrooms by ten, he told police. At around five the next morning, awoken by a heavy blow to the head, he discovered his father standing by his bed with an axe, mumbling incomprehensibly. After a struggle, Ronald had managed to wrench the axe away and force his father back into his bedroom, where he locked him in. He found his mother lying unconscious on her bed in a pool of blood, her face badly battered. A servant girl in a back room had slept through the whole episode.

According to Dr Isbister, both Ronald and Helen Woodruff were in a critical condition. Helen had two compound fractures to her forehead from the back of the axe, and was not expected to live. Ronald, who had a fractured skull and concussion, was not quite so gravely injured. Both were taken by ambulance to nearby Glengarlen private hospital in Lytton Street.

Mackay Woodruff, meanwhile, had been all but forgotten. Dr Isbister assumed that he was still safely locked in his bedroom, but when two police constables arrived at the cottage at around 6 a.m. they found no trace of him except a pool of blood on the floor and an open window. Bloodstains on the sill, and bloody tracks, led them to where Woodruff was lying on the grass some sixty feet from the cottage, naked and bleeding from a gash to the throat and cuts to his wrists and leg. Nearby, thrown over a low fence, they found a bloody razor. Nevertheless, despite a substantial loss of blood, Woodruff was expected to live. When taken to the Royal North Shore Hospital, they reported, he was muttering something incoherent about trains.

A little over six weeks later, on 12 November 1913, Mackay Woodruff appeared at Darlinghurst Criminal Court and was charged with feloniously wounding with intent to murder his wife and son. At his trial at the Central Criminal Court before Mr Justice Ferguson on 25 November, defended by the prominent barrister Sidney Mack, instructed by Norton Smith and Co., he pleaded not guilty. The Prosecutor, a Mr Robinson, told the jury that Woodruff had admitted to the assault, and the only issue they had to decide was whether or not he was sane when the crime was committed. Woodruff—now fifty-six, a squarely-built man of medium height and mild features, with blue eyes and greying black hair—spent most of his time leaning forward in the dock with one hand over his face, a journalist observed.

Sidney Mack's defence of Mackay Woodruff hadn't proven one of his finest hours, according to the press. Twenty-two-year-old Ronald was called as first witness. Ronald, who gave his address as Wallis Street in Woollahra, testified that his father, otherwise kind and attentive, had seemed 'a little strange and low-spirited' the previous night. He had been upset by an anonymous pamphlet circulated a few weeks before, said Ronald, although it had nothing to do with him or his business at all.

Dr Isbister next told the court that when he had seen Mackay Woodruff in the garden at Kyellah around six the next morning, he was satisfied that he was insane and had no comprehension of what was happening. Police Constable George Wright also testified that Woodruff was rambling and incoherent when found, and he couldn't understand anything he said.

At the North Shore Hospital, Constable Wright continued, Woodruff had told him he had woken in the night and got into a fight and found an axe to protect himself. On being informed (mistakenly) that wife and son were dead, he said that he wished he was dead too. A little later, 'wanting to relieve his mind', he had confessed to Wright that he had got up in the dark and, on seeing an axe by the woodshed, a 'mad fit' had come over him and he had gone into his son's room in a burst of fury, intending to maim him. He had hit his wife as she was getting out of bed. He had been suffering from mental troubles, he said, due to a circular being sent out about his business partnership.

Closing his case, Mr Mack asked Justice Ferguson to direct the jury to acquit the accused on the ground of insanity—Dr Isbister's evidence, he argued, was conclusive on this. Before the events, Woodruff had lived happily with his wife and son, and the wild and unnatural passion that had actuated his attack meant he was not responsible for his actions.

The jurors, however, were less convinced. After conferring among themselves they complained to the judge that they felt they had not heard enough evidence to justify a verdict of insanity. Mr Mack called an additional witness, a Mr John Keen, who related that in a conversation they had in the Blue Mountains the previous Saturday, Woodruff had told him that his business partner had 'something wrong with his head'.

'A little tap on the forehead with the back of an axe'—tapping his own temple—'that will put him right,' Woodruff had said. While obviously sober at the time, Woodruff seemed to Keen 'depressed and queer', and had further remarked that 'they all wanted fixing', and had also mentioned 'a vision from God'. Keen was similarly convinced that Woodruff was not in his right mind.

Despite this additional testimony, the *Daily Telegraph* reported, the jury remained uneasy. A juror asked whether Woodruff's state of mind had been 'tested by the proper authorities', or whether they must settle the question of it themselves.

Mr Justice Ferguson told the jury that it was for them to say, based on the evidence before them, if Woodruff were insane. He made it clear that if Woodruff were acquitted he would be detained in custody in a lunatic asylum. One juror still held out, but thirty-five minutes later they returned with a verdict of 'not guilty on the ground of insanity'. Mr Ferguson directed that Woodruff be kept as an insane patient at Darlinghurst Gaol 'until the Governor's Pleasure was known'. In the event, this was until 12 June 1915, two years later, when Woodruff was released from Goulburn Gaol and went to New Zealand with his wife Helen.

Again, this was not quite the end of the story. Ronald Woodruff, who also left for New Zealand to become a salesman with an Auckland mercantile firm, later deposed that he encountered his father again four years on, while his mother Helen was visiting her daughters in Sydney for ten months. In November 1919 at the Waverley Hotel in Auckland, Mackay Woodruff, now sixty-three and living at Whakatane, had once more seemed depressed and worried by financial matters, although again there seemed little reason for it. Early in the morning of 9 December Woodruff had left the hotel room he was sharing with a commercial traveller, climbed over a balustrade in the light well of the three-storey Endean's building at the corner of Queen and Quay Streets, and threw himself off. The Auckland Coroner, who conducted the inquest that followed, arrived at the opinion that he had done so while temporarily insane.

SIXTEEN

The Inquest

Christmas was a warm time of year, and Dr Stratford Sheldon's report to the Coroner after the autopsy was suitably prompt. His investigations of Wednesday 22 December 1920 had revealed that Claude's fatal injuries were caused by, firstly, a bullet to the back of the head. This bullet had been recovered from near the roof of the nose, and the wound displayed neither gunpowder marks nor singeing, reported Sunday's *Truth*. Another bullet had perforated Claude's head on the front right-hand side, within the hairline and a little above the right ear, extensively fracturing the skull. This wound, however, was surrounded by powder residue for a distance of about two inches. A corresponding exit wound was found opposite, above and behind the left ear.

A third bullet had entered Claude's chest. Dr Sheldon recorded that his colleague, Arthur Palmer, had told him that on first inspecting the body at Ingelbrae he had undone Dr Tozer's coat and waistcoat, and afterwards refastened them. Reopening the waistcoat at the Mortuary, Sheldon had noted a hole in the shirtfront with blackened and powder-stained edges. Below this was a single bloodstain about the size of a shilling. Undoing the shirt, he had located corresponding holes in the undershirt, which was open and doubled back at the flap.

Beneath these holes was a wound to the chest, slightly above the left nipple. Here the bullet had grazed the fourth rib and perforated the upper lobe of the right lung, causing substantial bleeding into the chest cavity. This bullet had exited at the back, above the tenth rib, where there was a corresponding hole in the back of the coat. Here the clothes were saturated with blood.

However, Dr Sheldon recorded, there was no hole in the waistcoat, nor in the front of the coat, which was fastened by its bottom button. Both of these had remarkably little blood on them, although the coat button and buttonhole were lightly blood-smeared, as were the waistcoat's front edges and buttonholes. The back of Dr Tozer's right hand was also lightly smeared with blood, but the palm was clear of gunpowder. This smearing of blood on the hand extended to the edge of the coat sleeve, which had been pulled up a little. The left hand was similarly smeared.

Claude's body was fully clothed, including his soft collar and tie and gold pin, and his wristlet watch was still keeping time at 4.10 p.m. A trickle of blood from his mouth indicated that the body had been lying on its right side. The corpse was already decomposing, but except for a part adhesion of the right lung to the chest wall, all the internal organs were healthy. Some partly-digested food was found in the stomach, probably fruit, but there was no smell of alcohol or sign of drugs. There was an old scar from an appendicitis operation.

Dr Sheldon had also observed an older scar at the inner angle of the left eye, under which was an old wound to the skull. Here he had discovered a piece of metal embedded at the base of the brain, which, he thought, had probably been there for years.

※

On Tuesday 28 December, according to the *Daily Telegraph*, Mrs Mort's condition remained serious. On the same day, a week after Claude's death, Detective Inspector Leary, in company with Superintendent Bannan, the Chief stipendiary magistrate and a deposition clerk, visited Dorothy in the North Shore Hospital and charged her with murder.

Dorothy, who made no reply to this, was remanded to appear before the City Coroner in ten days' time. On that date, 6 January 1921, she proved too ill to attend, and was remanded for a further week. The following day, chaperoned by special constable Nellie McGrath, Dorothy was driven by motorcar to the State Reformatory for Women at Long Bay. This measure allowed her to avoid the indignity of the Police Department tram, specially fitted inside with small wire-doored cells. In the prison's hospital ward—which *Truth* described as an airy, verandahed building decorated with fresh-cut flowers from the prison gardens—Dorothy was given a room to herself. It was now three weeks since Claude's death.

On 14 January, when a further party of police, lawyers and newspapermen visited her in the gaol hospital, Dorothy was sitting up in a chair beside her bed, fully dressed and attentive, and even able to smile once or twice, a newspaper recorded. Nevertheless, she was remanded for another fourteen days.

On 28 January, however, journalists at the special court convened at her bedside found her condition much worsened. Now lying in bed behind a screen with her eyes closed, Dorothy was barely able to answer questions. She appeared thin and haggard, with sunken eyes and a deathly pallor, and displayed 'signs of having undergone great suffering', it was reported. Since her previous remand she had been bedridden and slept very little. After proceedings lasting little more than a minute she was remanded for a fourth time, until 25 February. She whispered 'thank you'.

Just under a month later, when Dorothy had been in gaol some six weeks, the same official party was surprised to find her sitting up in a cane chair, wearing a fetching boudoir cap and making a small garment in wool or silk. According to the press, she sat up for a few hours each day, reading or knitting for her children, whose photograph stood on her locker. Despite this, at their arrival she became deathly pale and, when the charge was read out, trembled violently and seemed to swoon. Still appearing emaciated, she was remanded a fifth time, for another three weeks.

Dorothy's health continued to fluctuate. On 11 March, when Arthur Leary visited again, she denied knowing who he was. She also professed no recollection of what she had written in her letters or (among other events) of selling her brooch to the jeweller Beattie.

The inquest before the City Coroner, Mr John

Jamieson, finally took place few days later, on Monday 14 March, nearly three months after Claude's death. Dorothy arrived at the small, elegant Victorian sandstone Central Police Court in Liverpool Street by car at eight in the morning, chaperoned—as was customary with female offenders—by a white-robed gaol matron. By 8.30 a.m. a curious few had gathered on the steps beneath the pillars, hoping to catch a glimpse of her, but Dorothy and her chaperone had been met by Detective Constable Wickham, a burly six-footer from the Metropolitan Police, who escorted them to an inside room to wait for the case to begin at ten o'clock.

By nine-thirty, however, such a throng had gathered on the tiled courthouse verandah that half a dozen extra police were called in to supervise. The press in the intervening time had reported at length on the case, and now, when the iron doors finally opened for Dorothy's first public appearance, people trod on each others' feet and jostled for seats, leaving half the crowd still milling outside. Inside the small, drab courtroom, with its brown walls and elaborately-carved wooden canopy above the magistrate's bench, the atmosphere quickly became stifling.

After eleven weeks in custody, wrote a journalist, Dorothy seemed to be wasting away. Dressed entirely in black with a matching voluminous veil over her head, she was led to a large armchair, where she was carefully seated with cushions behind her head and a screen between her and the crowd in the public stalls at the back. Mary Ann Paulette, the gaol matron, was seated beside her. The press were gathered on benches at the side of the room, where their vision was not obscured. Once she was settled, the *Sun* reported, Dorothy seemed listless and weary and lay back with her eyes closed. Mrs Paulette fanned her briskly.

The legal counsel were already at their table in front of the bench. The police prosecutor Roderick Robert Kidston, instructed by Detectives Leary and Ramsay, was at his place to assist the Coroner. Later regarded as one of the finest prosecutorial minds in the state, at this stage Rod Kidston was a young barrister of twenty-nine, and only recently returned to his home in Mosman from service as a gunner overseas. Appearing for Dorothy was Sidney Mack KC, the senior barrister who had defended Dorothy's father in 1913, this time instructed by the solicitors Bradley, Son and Maughan. Assisting Mr Mack was Charles G. Addison, a solicitor and Mort family friend. Mr Selwyn Frederic Betts, instructed by Messrs Piggot and Stinson, represented Dr Tozer's family, while a Mr H.S. Bland was appearing for the Australian Provincial Insurance Company.

In their separate male and female holding rooms the witnesses—Florence Fizelle; neighbours George Kenworthy and William Smaillie; doctors Arthur Palmer, Stratford Sheldon, James Murray and Robert Lee-Brown; police officers Marden and Leary; Dorothy's drama teacher Lily Rock Phillips, the gunsmith William Cowles, the jewellery assistant William Beattie, the pharmacist James Johnstone; and finally Beatrice Tozer and Harold Mort—waited to be called. Among the exhibits to be tendered were six letters found at Ingelbrae on the night of Claude's death, and the manuscript of a play.

The object of a Coroner's inquest being only to

throw light on the circumstances surrounding a death, a Coroner has powers to accept evidence that would be ruled inadmissible elsewhere. Two among these attendant witnesses, Harold Mort—who could not be compelled to give evidence against his wife in a criminal court—and Lily Rock Phillips, would not be called upon to testify again at the trial, at which Harold's deposition would be read for him.

And so the journalists present busied themselves with their shorthand notes, later to be reconstructed with varying degrees of accuracy for the daily papers. Early in the proceedings, noted one, when Constable Marden spoke of the alleged shooting, Dorothy appeared to collapse in a faint. Court attendants rushed to remove her veil, and Mrs Paulette, seated at her side, fanned her vigorously, with no effect. Constable Wickham—tall, blond and blue-eyed—was again called upon.

'He lifted her frail form bodily out of the chair and carried her outside', reported the *Sun* with an obvious eye for pathos, while the Coroner himself remarked on the heavy atmosphere in the room.

Mr Kidston proposed that the idle curiosity seekers be asked to leave, and John Jamieson agreed. However no one moved. The Coroner remarked that he would ask the police to clear the court if they would not go willingly, but the idea came to nothing. While Dorothy was administered restoratives in an adjoining room, the two Counsels agreed to proceed without her.

The nearest approach to levity during a long morning came when the neighbour William Smaillie testified that he and his wife had arrived at Ingelbrae at 8.30 p.m. to find the front door open and Mrs Mort lying unconscious in her bedroom. Having seen the state of affairs, said Mr Smaillie, he had called the police.

'Did you have any conversation with her?' asked Mr Addison.

'No,' said Smaillie.

'Did she appear to you to be under considerable emotion?'

'Well,' answered Mr Smaillie, 'she *was* unconscious.'

By midday the crowd outside was no longer so large, noted the *Sun*, but many still could not get into the public gallery when the court resumed following the lunchtime adjournment. Dorothy was still absent, and the learned counsel again decided to carry on without her.

Harold Mort took the stand, wearing a dark formal coat and starched white butterfly collar. Tall, with thinning hair and a face lined by anxiety, he spoke at times with a catch in his voice and eyes that glistened with tears, reported *Truth*, but otherwise remained calm. His wife and he had been married for twelve years, he told Mr Kidston, and their two children were five and eight. Dr Tozer had been treating his wife for her nervous trouble for about six months, and it was he himself who had first called him in. The night before the events, because his wife was unwell, he had telephoned Dr Tozer and asked him to come in the morning. That day, after leaving at 9 a.m., he had received no messages, neither at his office nor at the University Club. Returning at about 10.30 p.m., he had found his home full of neighbours and police.

Dorothy, who had been in bed for several days, had

been feeling very low that morning, he reported. They had 'discussed things' the previous day, and while her conversation and demeanour were 'not ordinary', she seemed rational. Her mind, to him, was not unlike it had been for the previous year.

Questioned by Sidney Mack, Harold related that in late 1913, during her father's trial for attempted murder, Dorothy had been the only relative available to bear the brunt of it. She had suffered a nervous breakdown while the trial was pending, and another one, very severe, about three years later. Then, from December 1919, following her father's death from suicide earlier the same month, she had suffered from fits of depression. Dr Bell, her previous doctor, had told him that he had had to give her drugs for fear that she would break down again. She had experienced another such breakdown around the end of October last year. Since early November she had been distinctly morbid, and habitually spoke of suicide.

'Since then,' Harold continued, 'I was never sure whether I would find her alive or not.'

Mr Mack asked Harold if he had had any idea of any improper relations between his wife and Dr Tozer, but the Coroner interrupted him. 'The witness need only answer that if he likes,' he said. Mr Mack responded that he thought the witness would have no objection.

'I had no idea whatever,' Harold told the court. 'Since the tragedy my wife has discussed it with me, but I would rather not say what was said.'

Queried further on this point, Harold replied that he'd had many conversations with his wife since that day, and some days she seemed in her right mind, and at other times not. 'I don't think much reliance can be placed on what she says now,' he said.

'In the light of recent events, you know now that she was not rational at the time of the tragedy?' asked Mr Mack.

'Yes,' said Harold.

'Even when she was in a bad state, could you generally rely on the things she would say?' asked Mr Jamieson.

'Up to December, however depressed my wife was, I've never known her to make statements which I had any reason to doubt,' said Harold. 'Since December, I'm not in a position to be so sure.'

Lillian Rock Phillips related that in the six months from June to November 1920, Dorothy had come to her in Manly on two evenings a week to study drama. Their last contact had been about a fortnight before Claude's death. To play the leading role of 'Helen Madderson' in a sketch called 'Back Fire', said Lily, Mrs Mort had had to load a gun for her stage husband to shoot himself with. A very highly-strung and eccentric woman, she had bought a toy pistol to use in rehearsals, and had spoken of bringing her own revolver.

'I told her, if necessary, I will provide a pistol,' Lily continued.

'And does the husband finally shoot himself in the play?' asked Mr Mack.

'No. The husband shoots her lover,' said Lily. 'The woman wants to have them both, the husband for his money, and the lover because she loves him. After the lover is shot, the woman drops onto his dead body.'

(Here, *Truth* substituted, 'after shooting herself first'.)

Dr Robert Lee-Brown, the prison medical officer at Long Bay, gave evidence that Mrs Mort had now been under his care for nine weeks. Several weeks ago, he said, he had examined her at her own request to discover if she was pregnant.

'Did *she* say she was pregnant?' asked Mr Betts.

'She thought there might be a possibility,' replied Dr Lee-Brown, 'but she did not say she was.'

When the last witness had been examined, Dorothy, walking with slow, uneven steps, was escorted back to her armchair behind the screen. Mr Mack told the Coroner that she did not wish to call evidence.

'I would rather hear Mrs Mort say it,' Mr Jamieson said. 'Dorothy Mort, do you desire to give evidence at this inquest?'

An intense silence fell in the room, but no sound came from behind Dorothy's heavy black veil. Sidney Mack approached and spoke to her, but still she seemed unable to make herself heard. Consulting her again, Mr Mack conveyed her reply—'On the advice of my counsel, no.'

Mr Jamieson delivered his finding. Claude Tozer had died at Lindfield on 21 December 1920 from a bullet wound in the head, feloniously and maliciously inflicted by Dorothy Mort, who had murdered him. He committed her to stand trial for murder at the Central Criminal Court in Darlinghurst on 21 March, in a week's time.

At the Coroner's words, reported the *Herald*, Dorothy fell back in a swoon. Detective Wickham once again picked her up and carried her from the room, her arms dangling loosely. To avoid the crowd still gathered outside, a car was waiting at a rear entrance to take her back to Long Bay.

Claude's four love letters to Dorothy, found by Constable Marden in her bedroom on the night of 21 December, were printed in full next day in the *Sydney Morning Herald*. Alongside these appeared extracts from Dorothy's two unposted letters to Helen Woodruff and Beatrice Tozer. The public was allowed to digest that just before finishing her letter to her mother on 15 December, Dorothy had gone to the city and bought a .32 Colt automatic pistol.

'I feel ill again tonight, and have a feeling that I am going across to the other side soon. I am a real failure—doing things that I am sorry for after,' Dorothy wrote to Helen Woodruff.

I cannot be happy in my home. Everything is dust and ashes in my mouth, and I live in a perpetual state of nerves. Should anything happen to me, darling, will you always look after my darling children. They would be happier with you than with me, because lately I have not been able to give my whole heart to them, but I adore them all the same.

Dr Tozer was here this morning, and comes tomorrow. He swore to make me care for him as he cares for me, which he has done. I love and worship him to the exclusion of everything. He asked me to marry him and to later on get a divorce, but there were the children. I tried so hard to be strong and fine. He begged me so to be everything to him. For months I held out, and then one day he just forgot everything, and now we are eating our hearts out. Life is bitter hell, and I feel I cannot go on living. We love each other more and more. There was no going back once having crossed the Rubicon.

Today we agreed that we must not go on any longer. We say goodbye tomorrow, but will still meet as pals, which I don't think is possible. He said I was an angel, and how he reverenced me. What an incentive I'd been in all his work and play. How he loved me. He looked ghastly and is coming tomorrow to finally say goodbye. We know it is only right. He has been the most wonderful and perfect lover, but I cannot spare his life. May God forgive me. Goodbye my precious Mum. It is history repeating itself. I cannot help attracting men, as this last year has proved, but I never thought or meant to be wicked.

Ever your devoted daughter,
Dorri

In this partial transcription, the last paragraph—in which Dorothy had apparently, and rather startlingly, confided to her mother her intention to kill Claude—was marked 'Later' (and probably added on 19 December, the day she wrote to Beatrice). However, in the version given in the afternoon *Sun* of 22 December 1920, and again in *Truth* on 20 March 1921, the fourth last sentence reads 'but I cannot *spoil* his life'. No copy survives in the court transcript.

A few days after beginning this letter Dorothy had composed another, this time to Claude's mother, but again had not posted it.

'Your son has loved me, and I think more perfectly and wonderfully than is permitted to most people,' she wrote.

Mrs Mort's Madness

He forgot, as his recent letter says he might, and we agreed to part. I have twice asked him to let me release him, but he will not have it. Without any word or warning, or even suggestion, he asked another girl to marry him and then tells me, and says that the worst of it is that he loves me too; but he feels things are hopeless between us. Had he told me first, and then asked this girl to be his wife, I would have at once given him his freedom. For five wonderful months he has made me happy, begging me to trust him, as I implicitly did. I have been a most unhappy woman, and from our first meeting he loved me and swore to make me care. The shock I cannot survive. There are more cowardly things than taking one's life, and that is treachery to a woman, a trusting woman. One of the last wonderful things he said to me—"First I want your love, Di, then your soul, and lastly your body". He suggested divorce, but neither of us could bear that, but he said he would wait for me, and that he was content to do so. He looks ghastly and says how unhappy he really is, but it is too late.

This letter was signed 'Diana Mort'.

SEVENTEEN

The Trial: the First Day

> Wan, haggard, delicate to the point of fragility! Surely no more pathetic figure than that of Dorothy Mort ever sat behind the bars of a criminal dock in Australia ... More than half an hour before the court was due to open the public accommodation was fully occupied, and the big iron and stone doors were firmly closed in the face of many who waited without in the persistent drizzle ... A goodly number of those within ... were women, many of them habitués who make it a point never to miss the spectacle of some person fighting for liberty or honour ...
>
> —*Daily Telegraph,* 8 April 1921

Mr Mack, it was said, was the Man for Murder.

An untidy, deceptively mild-looking man with light hazel eyes and a monocle that lent him a bookish air, Sidney Mack had first made his name as a criminal barrister in 1901 during the sensational trial of Jane Smith. An ex-barmaid, Smith was acquitted of poisoning a middle-aged butcher from whom she had inveigled a sum of money. The crime, committed on board a ship from New Zealand, was almost perfect, except that the victim was not (as Mrs Smith had anticipated) buried at sea, and strychnine was discovered in the body during a post-mortem. With Mr Mack defending, Smith underwent three separate trials, at the end of each of which—after long and passionate final addresses from the defence—the jury was unable to reach a verdict. Generous, erratic, charming, outspoken, and unreliable, Sid Mack had brought himself to further attention at the time by bringing contempt charges against several newspapers.

One of thirteen children of an impoverished Wesleyan minister who had migrated to the Araluen goldfields, Sidney had grown up with his large and peripatetic family—his siblings included Louise Mack, the romantic novelist, and Amy Mack, a well-known *Women's Weekly* editor and children's author—in a string of rowdy Bohemian households in Balmain, Newtown and Redfern. The roots of his unconventional attitude to affairs of the heart lay in his student days, when he had become secretly engaged to a young woman whose father forbade their marriage. Now approaching fifty, Mr Mack had been appointed a King's Counsel just two years before.

The Crown Prosecutor, Mr William Thomas Coyle KC, and Sidney Mack had gone head to head a number of times before. After studying law at the University of Sydney in the early 1890s, both until recently had had rooms at Selborne Chambers in Phillip Street. A bull-shouldered man several years older than Mr Mack, William Coyle, the son of a publican who became prosperous on the Sofala diggings, had been educated at St Ignatius College and Riverview, where he excelled at rowing and rugby. But if Coyle and

Mack were both progeny of Irish immigrants to the goldfields, there the similarities ended. Appointed the state's first Senior Crown Prosecutor in August 1920, some seven months before, Coyle's characteristically genial expression was known to mask a formidable intellect. Calm, methodical, and always reliant on carefully-reasoned legal argument (although not above the occasional impressive literary flourish in a final address), Mr Coyle had quickly established a reputation for unsettling defence counsels with his adversarial tenacity and sardonic manner.

'Court philosophy is that Mr Coyle is most dangerous when he smiles,' quipped a newspaper columnist, '... [and] rare indeed is the day when Mr Coyle does not smile. Mr Coyle really cannot help it. Possibly he came smiling into a smiling world.'

William Coyle might also have had his own reasons for an interest in the idiosyncrasies of the fairer sex. As a law student at Sydney University he had kept company with an older woman who, in the early 1890s, had allegedly tried to entrap him into marriage. On his declining her advances she had brought a charge against him, which was quickly dismissed—but the young Coyle took the precaution of accompanying his mother to England to further his studies at the Inner Temple, where he stayed until 1902.

In a city of just over a million people, it was inevitable that most of the other personalities involved in Dorothy's trial knew each other. Residing in Holt Street in Double Bay, William Coyle—while a Catholic himself—would have been familiar with the family of Canon Mort, living just up the hill in Woollahra. The Chief Justice Sir William Cullen, who lived at Balmoral on the north side, was a founder and (as the state's Lieutenant Governor) Patron of the Royal North Shore Hospital, and thus also well acquainted with the doctors who had treated Dorothy there the previous year.

North Shore Hospital superintendent Dr Emma Albani Buckley, a witness for the defence, had been a schoolteacher as a young woman, and by her own account had known Dorothy for eighteen years. Now forty-one, she had graduated in medicine at Sydney in 1911, and so inevitably would also have known Claude Tozer from her student days, although she gave no public indication of it.

Dr Erasmus Bligh, another prominent defence witness and well-known consultant surgeon at Royal North Shore, had gained his degree in 1905, and thus had attended Sydney University at the same time as Harold Mort. Now living at Wollstonecraft—in addition to his Macquarie Street rooms he had a practice at Miller Street, North Sydney—he too had encountered Dorothy as a schoolgirl. Eight years earlier, at Glengarlen hospital in North Sydney, he had also treated Helen and Ronald Woodruff for their injuries inflicted by Dorothy's father.

Without the intervention of *Truth* newspaper of Sunday 26 December 1920, however, few people might have connected the two cases until now—except, of course, for Dorothy's defence counsel Mr Sidney Mack KC, who had defended Mackay Woodruff at his trial for attempted murder.

❧

Rain swept the steps of the Central Criminal Court in Darlinghurst on the morning of Thursday 7 April 1921 when Dorothy Mort was finally brought to trial. Three weeks had passed since her appearance before the Coroner, and nearly a hundred onlookers, wrapped in overcoats and carrying umbrellas, had gathered under the carved stone lion and unicorn above the portal. When the massive iron doors finally swung open, well-dressed women—'of the novel reading type', according to *Truth*—packed the upper gallery, while the public enclosure downstairs quickly filled with men. Those left outside in the wet forecourt kept on waiting, hoping to find a seat as the day wore on.

Inside the courtroom, the atmosphere was again uncomfortably close. At two minutes past ten the Chief Justice Sir William Cullen entered, formidable in his scarlet robes and full white wig. He was closely followed by Sidney Mack in the customary black. The Prosecutor William Coyle, his broad, florid face a marked contrast to his delicate bands of Irish lace, also took his seat.

'The King versus Dorothy Mort! Call Dorothy Mort!' came the cry.

The journalists sat to attention. At seven minutes past ten precisely, Dorothy was escorted in, again unrecognisable under a dark veil, her plain black dress stark against the gaol matron's white. Press opinion varied as to her state of mind and health. According to the *Sun*, although she seemed weak and ill, she entered unassisted and walked straight to the prisoner's dock, where she calmly took her seat. The *Daily Telegraph*, in contrast, felt she was clearly in a daze and seemed not to know where she was. To the *Sydney Morning*

Herald's writer she was frail and dejected, and sat as if spellbound, her eyes fixed on the floor.

Sidney Mack put his hand between the polished wooden bars and briefly shook her hand, evidently to reassure her. Called upon to plead, she stood motionless, apparently unable to speak despite two requests from the judge's associate. Finally Mr Mack rose again from the Counsel table and leaned over the railings.

'Say it,' he was heard to encourage her, but behind her veil Dorothy's lips evidently did not move. She was breathing heavily and appeared to be in the grip of great emotion, reported the *Sun*, and Mr Mack spoke to her in lowered tones for several minutes before turning and relaying her inaudible 'Not guilty' to the room.

A silence, described as grim, prevailed while the twelve male jurors were sworn in. None were challenged. Mr Mack, noting that his client had risen from her prison sickbed, suggested that she be allowed to be seated more comfortably.

'It seems almost inhuman that a woman so weak should sit in that dock,' he remarked, undoubtedly with an eye to the watching jurors.

Sir William Cullen permitted Dorothy to take a chair on the floor of the court, opposite her counsels Mr Mack and Mr Addison. A little later, recorded the journalists, she appeared to lose all strength, resting her head on the gaol matron's shoulder.

For three-quarters of an hour Mr Coyle opened the Crown case in his usual incisive manner. Mrs Mort was a married woman, apparently living happily with her husband, he began. The prosecution would show that relations existed between her and Dr Tozer that should not have existed between a married woman and a single man, and more especially when he was her medical attendant.

Letters would be produced to indicate that a passionate love had sprung up between them. The accused was highly-strung, of nervous temperament, and from the evidence of these letters—painful as it was to reveal; this was a painful case—a woman of strangely neurotic temper. Dr Tozer had won great distinction at the War, and as a cricketer and athlete, and perhaps this was part of his charm for her. And so, from July 1920, their friendship had ripened into love. From her own admissions, it was clear that illicit relations had occurred.

What had happened while the two were alone together on the morning of 21 December Mrs Mort herself had since related, and there was abundant evidence to support it. Some time before, Dr Tozer had concluded that it was neither well nor wise for a medical man to be unmarried. Accordingly, he had told Mrs Mort that he had made up his mind to wed, but had assured her that his affection for her remained unchanged. This revelation had affected her considerably, according to her own statements and letters, and she had determined that if she could not have him, neither should anyone else.

Six days before the tragedy, Mr Coyle went on, Mrs Mort had gone to Cowles and Dunn and bought an automatic pistol. Ostensibly it was a present for her husband, but she had asked for tuition in loading it. Mr Coyle picked up the weapon and held it up before the court. Beside Dorothy, the gaol matron raised her fan, blocking the pistol from her view.

Dr Tozer's letters to Dorothy had dated from the very month he began to visit her, Coyle continued, and he had written in one of them that 'the barriers were down' and that 'the only thing that would save them was her purity'.

'But,' declared the Prosecutor, 'her purity did *not* save them.'

Just as Mr Coyle was embarking on a description of Beatrice Tozer's bedside interview with Dorothy on the day following Claude's death, Mr Mack jumped to his feet. The Prosecution should not open with any such confession by Mrs Mort, he objected, because at that time she was insane, and any statement she made could not therefore have been a voluntary one.

'I suppose it will have to be placed before the jury at some time,' said Sir William Cullen.

'The Crown argues that she was quite sane,' said Mr Coyle.

Sir William Cullen, faced with the unusual gambit of the Defence raising an objection during the Prosecution's opening address, overruled it. Mr Mack sat down, no doubt satisfied that he had planted the defence of insanity in the jurors' minds at the earliest possible moment.

Mr Coyle quickly moved on to the deposition of special constable Nellie McGrath, who had guarded Dorothy at North Shore Hospital and afterwards accompanied her to Long Bay. Once again Mr Mack was on his feet. This evidence should also not be mentioned here, he said: the testimony had not been given at the Coroner's Court, but had been introduced at the last moment, and he questioned its admissibility.

Sir William Cullen allowed this objection, and a similar one to a deposition by Constable Alfred Marden.

Again Mr Coyle moved swiftly on. Medical evidence would indicate that the shots that had killed Dr Tozer were fired while his waistcoat was open, and that afterwards someone had buttoned it up. The defence, he suggested, would maintain that Mrs Mort was not sane when, after her own wounding, she had made certain statements. That was for the jury to decide. There was an abundance of motive. The onus now was on the accused to show that she was insane; but the jury would need to go far to conclude that she was not aware of what she was doing—or, if she was aware of it, that she did not know it was wrong.

'This is a painful case, painful on every side of it,' Mr Coyle repeated. 'The man did what he should not have done, and also the woman. The man is dead; the woman is alive. The mere fact that she is a woman is not to play on your judgement.'

Mrs Mort's Madness

'MISS FIZELLE
Who was lady companion to Mrs. Mort at the time of the tragedy.' Photo: *Daily Telegraph* 15 March 1921, page 5

When Florence Fizelle walked to the witness box, Dorothy lowered her head onto one hand. Miss Fizelle also wore a veil of black gossamer over her wide-brimmed hat, but lifted it at the Judge's direction. In an almost inaudible whisper she told the court that she was a single woman, now living at Warwilla Avenue, Wahroonga, and confirmed that she had been Mrs Mort's companion for seven months, until 21 December the previous year. On the morning of that day, she said, only she and Dorothy had been at home, and the children were playing outside, within sight of the house.

During the previous five months Dr Tozer had

visited fairly often; sometimes two or three times a week, and then not for several weeks. Sometimes he would stay a short time only, sometimes for over an hour. She had not been in the habit of entering Mrs Mort's room during his professional visits, she told Mr Coyle, but she did not remember him staying late when Mr Mort was away.

At this point in her testimony to the committal proceedings three weeks before, Miss Fizelle had revealed that medicine was delivered to the house after Dr Tozer's calls, but now neither the prosecution nor the defence revisited the observation.

On 21 December, Florence continued, Mrs Mort had been in poor health, melancholy and nervous, and physically weak. For the previous five days she had kept to her bed. After Dr Tozer's arrival, and after hearing what she believed to be a shot and finding the drawing room door locked, she had gone next door to telephone for Mr Mort to come home immediately. She had heard two more shots as she re-entered the house.

'After I heard what I think was the first shot I was not very much perturbed because I did not know it was a shot until I found the door locked, and then I began to get very frightened,' Miss Fizelle said. 'I don't remember anything more for a long time—I must have fainted. Next thing I remember I was on the verandah and one of the children was speaking to me. I have no idea what time that was, late afternoon. I attempted to rise, but was unable to do so.'

Recapping the events from sometime after three in the afternoon, when Mrs Mort had first asked for iced water, Florence recounted that although she had waited in the passage, her mistress did not unlock the drawing room door. On her return to the house at about five after playing outside with the children, she could hear Mrs Mort pacing about in her bedroom. Now, when spoken to, she no longer replied. After giving the children their tea and putting them to bed at seven, she had spoken to Dorothy again, and once again she asked for iced water.

Mrs Mort had fumbled at the door for a long time to get it open, said Florence. She herself had turned away down the passage, but then quickly came back, and despite Dorothy's efforts to shut her out, had pushed her way in.

'I could see that she had been wounded, and was in a demented condition and covered with blood. I wanted her to let me attend her wound, but she said nothing was the matter with her. I said there must be, there was so much blood. She said, "No, it is only a little haemorrhage." For a long time I tried to get her to bed, and she struggled, but at last she agreed to let me wash her. I got the bath heater going and ran next door and brought in Mr Wallace. No one else came for a long time. I came back and washed her as much as she would let me, just her face. I got her into bed several times, but she just got out again straight away,' said Miss Fizelle.

Here again the detail of Florence's evidence departed from her account three weeks before. 'When I got into the bedroom she was walking up and down like a wild woman,' Florence had told the Coroner's Court. 'She was clearly out of her mind, and fought me. She was talking wildly, and she struggled, although she did not try to hurt me. By humouring her, and saying that if I covered her up no one would see her wound, I got her into bed. She was trying to drink from everything she could get her hands on, even a candle stick—she did not seem to know what it was. She was right out of her mind at the time. There was no question of that.'

Later, said Florence to Mr Coyle, a constable had come and she had handed him some keys. He had found the one that unlocked the door to the dining room, which was curtained off from the drawing room, but had no wall between. She herself had not entered.

In answer to Mr Mack, Miss Fizelle outlined further instances of her mistress's aberrant behaviour. Sometime in June last year, she said, she had noticed that Dorothy was experiencing fainting fits. One of them, in November, had lasted several hours.

'Do you remember an incident one Sunday at the end of November, or in early December, when Mr Mort and the children were at church?' asked Mr Mack. 'Mrs Mort had been cleaning her gloves with benzine, which got on her hands and caught fire?'

'She kept saying the children were in flames, talking of the poor little children being burnt,' Florence agreed.

'You remember the bed taking fire?' asked Mr Mack.

'Yes. She was in hysterics for about five hours.'

'She kept saying the children were on fire, and was quite convinced of it?'

'Yes,' repeated Florence.

'Did she seem quite sane?'

'Not at that time.'

Afterwards, the attacks had come more frequently,

Mrs Mort's Madness

Miss Fizelle continued, and she was always dwelling on death. 'She would say, "I wish I were dead" or "I would like to die". On the night of 9 December, the anniversary of her father's death, she was very strange and despondent. That day seemed to have a marked effect on her. She would talk a great deal, but incoherently and would lose the thread of what she was saying. She didn't seem to be herself.'

'She spoke of committing suicide on that day?' asked Mr Mack.

'I wouldn't say that,' said Florence. 'She was morbid. She did not exactly say that she would go in the same way, but spoke of hereditary traits. She said how awful it must be for people who could not help to thinking of these things. I tried to persuade her of the folly of such talk, but she could never see anything wrong in it.'

'She thought it a meritorious thing, suicide, did she not?' asked Mr Mack.

'I don't know about that, but she couldn't see anything wrong in it,' said Florence.

Mr Mack asked Miss Fizelle if she were aware of the events preceding Mackay Woodruff's own suicide, but Mr Coyle objected and the question was withdrawn.

When Mrs Mort spoke of her own death, Florence reiterated, she would try to cheer her up. Dorothy was like a child at times, accepting any suggestion and repeatedly contradicting herself. On 19 December, a Sunday—the day she had written to Beatrice Tozer—her mind was in a haze, and she could not seem to see things that were handed to her, such as plates and other objects: she could not judge their distance away. Dorothy had talked a lot on that day.

On the night of 20 December, Florence went on, she

had heard a murmur of earnest conversation between Mr and Mrs Mort, but that in itself was not unusual.

'How did Dr Tozer look when you admitted him on the morning of December 21?' asked Mr Mack.

'He was rather pale,' said Florence. 'He looked bad.'

The two unposted letters to Helen Woodruff and Beatrice Tozer were produced, and Miss Fizelle identified Dorothy's handwriting. However, said Florence, at the time they were written Dorothy's condition was such that she would take no notice of anything in them.

Mr Coyle, for the prosecution, re-examined. Her mistress was not always in the state described, Florence agreed. 'Sometimes she was quite bright,' she acknowledged. Occasionally, Dorothy would take the children to picture shows in town: she was always very fond of her children.

'I was always on good terms with her, and had a great regard for her,' Miss Fizelle concluded.

Dr James Murray was next to take the stand. Now in his mid-sixties, Scottish-born and trained in Edinburgh, he had practised medicine for thirty years, he told the court. His experience in mental asylums included Fyfe Kinross in Scotland and—after arriving in Australia in 1908—Gladesville, Parramatta and Callan Park in New South Wales.

When he had examined Mrs Mort on the night of 21 December, he had found her partially comatose and suffering a bullet wound to her left breast. The bullet—similar to the one now produced in court—must have passed very close to her heart, and through the lung, before exiting close to the shoulder blade. This injury could have been self-inflicted. The blood around the wound was dry, with very little oozing, indicating that the injury was a good many hours old. More dried blood on her body suggested that she had been still for a considerable time, but then had moved about.

By midday next day she had recovered from the effects of the laudanum poisoning, but remained confused, and he was satisfied that she was of unsound mind. Knowing her family history, he told Mr Mack, he would say she had been deranged for a considerable time. And at that point, he said, the case had gone out of his hands.

Mr Mack, anxious to reinforce this aspect of the evidence in the minds of the jurors, pursued it at length. If her father had tried to murder his wife and son, and then tried to cut his own throat, and then—after a jury had judged him insane—had finally committed suicide, was it not probable that he would leave a hereditary taint in his daughter?

'Highly probable, although I formed the opinion she was mentally deranged before I knew of her family history,' Dr Murray replied. 'But then, if her father was homicidal and suicidal, it would be in keeping with what I saw. Now I have heard enough to make me sure there was probably some inherited brain trouble. I would say she was a woman of very neurotic temperament. With an inherited tendency, any external shock might be liable to make her unhinged.'

'Supposing she got news that her father had killed himself—would that shock, of hearing of his death, cause her to become deranged?' asked Mr Mack.

'I should imagine so,' said Dr Murray.

'And any other undue emotion would also be dangerous to a woman with her neurotic temperament and history?'

'A neurotic person should not be under emotional or passionate influences,' Dr Murray agreed. 'One of the main things is to calm the patient as much as possible, and avoid any excitement. In her state of mind, any sudden shock might send her off her balance—and particularly one that was the result of disappointed love.'

'What would not be dangerous to another, then, might be dangerous to her?' Mr Mack asked.

'It would be in keeping with what I saw,' Dr Murray repeated.

'And such a person, a person suffering from insanity, might imagine things that never happened?' Mr Mack said.

Dr Murray concurred.

Mr Coyle, cross-examining, came straight to the point. 'With regard to this suggested cause of emotion, do you think the death of Mrs Mort's father, twelve months before, influenced her conduct in December 1920?'

'It depends on when her mind became deranged,' said Dr Murray.

'The anniversary of that death, occurring on 9 December, might also be likely to affect her on December 21?' asked Mr Coyle.

'It is impossible to say,' said Dr Murray.

'Supposing a man conducted his business successfully—up to, say, the age of 57—and then suddenly became deranged, would you say that man, whose only brain failure it was, would leave an hereditary taint in his offspring?' asked Mr Coyle.

'There are few things more hereditary than insanity,' said Dr Murray. 'If a man became insane late in life, one would always suspect that the taint might have been transmitted, even if the derangement occurred only once.'

'Even when it occurred long after the birth of his children?' asked Mr Coyle.

'Yes.'

The Government Medical Officer Dr Arthur Aubrey Palmer confirmed the findings of his autopsy, conducted with Dr Sheldon on 22 December 1920: Claude Tozer's death had been caused by bullet wounds from a .32 calibre weapon, fired at close quarters.

With the chest wound, the shot had been fired from about two inches away, while Dr Tozer's waistcoat was open, he testified. That the coat and waistcoat were unmarked, while the shirt was singed and powder-stained, indicated that the waistcoat had later been buttoned up. The bullet to the right temple had similarly been fired from about two inches away.

With the wound to the back of the head, however, an absence of gunpowder stains suggested that here the gun had been fired from further away. The cause of death, Dr Palmer continued, was the two bullet wounds to the head, although the chest wound might have contributed. The deceased could have inflicted any of these wounds on himself, he felt, but not all three. The shot to the back of the head—fired from the greatest distance away—would be the hardest to self-inflict.

To questions from Mr Coyle, Dr Palmer further refined these conclusions. If the chest wound had come first, Dr Tozer could not have inflicted either of the head wounds himself, he believed. The back of the head would be an extraordinary place in which to shoot oneself, he added—and while it was *possible* that such a wound could be self-inflicted, it was highly improbable. The position of the weapon, when it was found, did not suggest that it had fallen from Dr Tozer's hand.

In answer to Mr Mack, Dr Palmer confirmed that he had seen Dorothy Mort at North Shore Hospital on 24 December, three days after Dr Tozer's death, while consulting with other doctors about her mental health. At that point, he believed that Dorothy was certifiably insane, and probably had been so for some time. It was not a condition she would get into suddenly.

'You might call it emotional insanity,' he responded to Mr Coyle. There were a number of kinds of insanity, but he knew her condition only as he saw it on that day.

When he entered her room, he continued, Dorothy had seemed highly excited. When he asked how she was getting along, she answered, 'Very well, but I won't have any blood drawn off.'

'I assured her we intended to do no such thing, and then she said, "I have been delayed in coming here by my husband. He kept me to measure me for a coffin,"' Dr Palmer went on. 'Holding her hands up, she exclaimed, "It was a very pretty little coffin, about that size"'—here Dr Palmer held up his own hands, about two feet apart—'and I think she said it had silver handles.'

Later, when Mrs Mort said she wanted to make a statement, he had advised her not to make it to him. He was a doctor, not a detective, he told her.

'She replied, "I simply wanted to say I shot Dr Tozer."

'Oh, you did, did you?' he answered.

'"Yes," she said, "I became pregnant to him, and I want to be examined by the doctor I saw before."

'I asked if she meant Dr Murray, and she said, "Yes—to see if the child is Dr Tozer's; for if it is, and Mrs Tozer wants it, she can have it."

'She spoke of all this in quite an ordinary way, and I was quite clear that she was incapable of understanding the nature and quality of her acts. She talked as if she had been speaking of the weather, and did not seem to be in the least upset,' said Dr Murray.

Constable Alfred Marden had been a teamster and timber-getter before joining the police force twenty years before and, despite now approaching middle-age, retained something of the build. Holding his notebook in his large hands, he took the court through the events of his arrival at Ingelbrae on 21 December and his observation of Dr Tozer's body in the drawing room at around 9.30 p.m. He went on to enumerate the various items he had discovered, including the Colt 'revolver' and empty cartridge shells, the bullet holes in the furniture and walls, and Dr Tozer's letters in Dorothy's bedroom.

Claude's four letters to Dorothy—already familiar to those present from the daily newspapers—were read aloud by the judge's associate. Constable Marden detailed how, in searching the bedroom, he had also found two empty cardboard boxes for automatic weapons and a box of bullets on a wardrobe shelf. When these last items were produced as exhibits, Dorothy's attendant, on whose shoulder Dorothy had been resting her head, and who had been supporting her with one arm, again raised her fan. Dorothy closed her eyes.

Some two weeks later on 6 January 1921, while he was on guard at the door of her North Shore Hospital ward between 5 and 6 p.m., Marden went on, Mrs Mort had called him over. Mr Mack jumped to his feet. 'On the evidence of the doctors, she was mad at this time. She was incapable of making a voluntary statement,' he exclaimed.

'But don't you see that this is for the jury to consider?' the Chief Justice said. 'I will note your objection, but allow the evidence to be given.'

'She said, "Come here, Sergeant, I want to speak to you",' continued Marden. 'I went to her bedside and she asked me, "Did you ever shoot anyone?"

'"No, never," I replied, and she said, "I did."'

He had warned her against saying this to him, he told the court, as it might be given in evidence against her, but Mrs Mort had replied, '"I don't mind. I am prepared to suffer any punishment the law might inflict."'

Again Constable Marden consulted his notebook.

'She said, "I shot Dr Tozer. He was sitting on the couch. I was standing behind, and showing him a little present I had bought for him in my left hand. I took the revolver from the ledge behind me in my right hand and shot him in the back of the head. I then went round the end of the couch and shot him through the side of the head. I afterwards undid his vest and shot him in the chest, and I buttoned up his vest afterwards. I am sorry. I don't know what made me do it. It was horrible. I wished I could die. I lay in his arms for two hours afterwards."

'When she made that statement, I could not say if her attitude was that she did not care what became of her,' said Constable Marden in response to Mr Coyle. 'She seemed quite rational to me.'

Detective Inspector 3rd Class Arthur Leary produced the crime scene photograph showing Claude Tozer's body lying in the drawing room at Ingelbrae; the blood-stained visiting card and the torn photograph of Dorothy he had found in a nearby waste paper basket; a heart-shaped locket, and an empty bottle. Both the bottle and Mrs Mort's stomach contents had been found to contain laudanum, he told the court.

When the photograph was pieced together, continued Leary, the writing on the back was deciphered to read: 'Claude Tozer. From the woman you swore you loved and reverenced above all others, and said was the highest incentive for good in your life. Di'. Beneath this was written, 'From the woman you loved and made the mother of your child'. Dr Tozer's visiting card, with the date 'December 4' written on it, also had on the back the words 'To my best pal Claude Tozer', but the rest was unintelligible. To Leary, the bloodstains on these two items indicated that both had been torn up and thrown away after Dr Tozer's death.

Five days after the events, Leary had visited Mrs Mort at Royal North Shore Hospital and formally charged her with murder. At this date she hadn't recognised him, although she said she knew she'd seen him before. On Friday 11 March, when he saw her again in the Long Bay hospital ward, again she said she didn't remember him. Shown two letters in her own handwriting, Mrs Mort had acknowledged they were hers, but said she couldn't remember now what she had written in them. After this interview, Leary continued, he had lined her up with five other women on chairs in the prison ward, and Mr Cowles the gunsmith and Mr Beattie the jeweller had picked her out immediately.

When he had inquired if she would like to put any questions to them, she'd said, 'Yes, the small man', and—pointing to Mr Beattie—asked, 'Do you say I sold you a brooch?' Mr Beattie had replied yes. 'It's strange, I can't remember that,' Dorothy had said when shown the brooch. When she was told she had sold it to him for five pounds, Leary related, Dorothy again said she could not recollect it. She had given the name 'Diana Reay', Mr Beattie reminded her.

'Oh yes,' she agreed, 'my nom-de-plume.'

EIGHTEEN

The Afternoon of the First Day

A buzz of expectation rose in the visitors' gallery as the first witness of the afternoon approached the stand. A tall and handsome woman with—according to *Truth*—a beautifully modulated voice, Beatrice Tozer recounted that she had last seen her son alive at Shireen, her house in Roseville, at around eleven on the morning of 21 December. After his visit to Dorothy Mort, Claude was to return to Roseville at lunchtime before going on to watch the Test match in the afternoon.

The first time she had met Mrs Mort was on the day after her son's death, Beatrice continued. On that day, 22 December, she had gone to Ingelbrae at Dorothy's request, and found her in bed. She appeared ill, but to her, Dorothy's manner seemed studied.

'She said, "Sit down. I feel that I am dying, and I want you to know the whole truth",' Beatrice said. 'She told me, "For two years before I met Dr Tozer I was desperately unhappy, for reasons I need not go into now. When I fell ill and my husband called the doctor in, I loved him immediately I saw him."'

'She said to me, "He was so handsome, so big and splendid. I thought how wonderful a son of his would be. Last year I bought a revolver for a man going to Morocco, but I hadn't given him all the cartridges. This year I bought another one, and with these I shot the doctor."

'"How did you do it?" I asked her.

'She said, "I went up close to him and he died immediately. He did not suffer."'

Here alone, a journalist wrote, Mrs Tozer's self-control broke down and her voice betrayed a tremor.

'If you loved him, why did you kill him?' Beatrice asked.

Dorothy had hesitated, Mrs Tozer told the court, and then said, '"We talked it over together and decided it was the only way out".

'I said, "Tell me the truth, if you are dying; you know that he had no intention of taking his own life, or yours."'

At this, said Beatrice, Dorothy had cried out and then answered her, '"I will tell you the truth. Last time he came here he told me he had come to the conclusion that it was better for a medical man to be married, and that he intended asking some girl to be his wife. It was too cruel. I could not bear it, and I determined that if I could not have him no other woman should."'

Mrs Mort had then asked her to kiss her and forgive her, said Beatrice, and that was all she had said.

To Mr Coyle, Mrs Tozer acknowledged that her son had been treating Dorothy for hysteria and neurasthenia for some time, and that he visited her fairly often.

'Sometimes every day of the week?' asked Mr Coyle.

'Well, very often,' replied Beatrice, 'depending on whether or not she was ill.'

From his appointment book, which she herself had kept, said Beatrice, Claude had seen Mrs Mort, or her little boy, at Ingelbrae fifteen or sixteen times over five months, starting from 23 June. When Dorothy rang for him, it was mostly she who took the calls. If her son was out, sometimes he would respond later, and she'd heard him answering 'Yes' and 'No' over the telephone. In her hearing, he had never expressed an intention of taking own his life.

On the night of 21 December, Beatrice told Mr Mack, he had arranged to go to the theatre—'He had already bought the tickets,' she said.

'With whom?' asked Mr Mack.

'A friend,' replied Beatrice.

'Was it a lady friend—the lady to whom he was engaged?' asked Mr Mack.

'My son,' said Beatrice, 'was not engaged.'

Next on the stand was James Johnstone, of W. G. Cains Ltd, Dispensing and Shipping Chemists, 45 Pitt Street in the city. Johnstone lived at McMahon's Point, he told the court, and knew Mrs Mort because they had both belonged to the same dramatic club. She had called at his shop only once, on 2 December last year, and after some general conversation had remarked that—'bye the bye'—she wanted some laudanum. He had asked her what she was going to do with it.

'She told me she had been reading a doctor's book that advised the use of it with olive oil for earache, and said that she wanted some for her son. I sold her a six drachm phial labelled "Laudanum (Tincture of Opium)" and "Poison",' Mr Johnstone continued. A fatal dose, he said, was about fifteen minims.[1]

'I said to her quite casually, "Mrs Mort, you must not get to drinking it", and she replied, "Would it hurt me—that much?"

'I told her, "There is quite sufficient there to kill everyone in the house."'

In answer to Mr Mack, Johnstone responded that his own mother had used the same remedy—olive oil and laudanum, warmed in a spoon and poured into the ear—when he was a boy. 'I was quite satisfied that she was going to use it for that purpose,' he said. He had entered the purchase in the poison register, Mrs Mort had signed it, and he had not seen her again until now.

William Beattie, jewellery assistant at the Mont de Piété at 77 Castlereagh Street in the city, confirmed that on Wednesday 15 December 1920 he had bought a brooch—the one now tendered in court—from Mrs Mort.

'She wanted ten pounds for it, and said she had had it valued at Fairfax and Roberts for that,' he said. 'I told her it was only worth five to me. I gave her five pounds for it, and she signed a receipt. Afterwards I identified her at the State Reformatory.'

William Charles Walter Cowles, of Cowles and Dunn in King Street, recalled that on the same day a

---

[1] 15/480 —or 1/32nd —of an imperial fluid ounce

woman in white had visited his business and asked to see an automatic pistol. She wanted to post it to her husband, she said, who was travelling in India with the author Ralph Stock.

They'd had a long conversation, Cowles said. He had shown her the workings of a .32 Colt automatic pistol—the one now exhibited—and she had manipulated the pistol with dummy cartridges, and bought it, although she'd purchased no cartridges at the time. 'She had to hunt around in her purse to find the money, and gave me small silver and copper to make up the amount,' he added. When Inspector Leary had showed him the pistol again it had three live cartridges in it, with one in the barrel.

Mary Clare McGrath—now Mrs Nellie Manktelow of Denham Street, Bondi—testified that before her recent marriage she had been a special constable of police. A forthright young woman in her early thirties, she said that on 26 December, two days after she had taken up duty watching over Mrs Mort at North Shore Hospital, Mrs Mort had called her over. As she was wearing civilian clothing, how were people to know she was a policewoman, Dorothy had wanted to know. Nellie had produced her warrant card, and later that day Mrs Mort had asked her if she had ever shot anyone.

'If you ever want to shoot someone, always use an automatic pistol; they always shoot straight,' Dorothy had told her.

'"Not in your case,"' answered Nellie.

There was a stir in the court at this, wrote the journalists, and Dorothy collapsed into the arms of the gaol matron. Mr Mack jumped to his feet. Mrs Manktelow's remark was an inducement, he exclaimed. Sir William Cullen overruled his objection, and Dorothy—again being vigorously fanned by her attendant—seemed oblivious to everything. When the court had settled, Nellie continued.

'Mrs Mort replied, "With myself, yes, but it was different with Dr Tozer, I shot him,"' said Nellie. 'She went on to tell me how she did it. I warned her not to talk like that, but she said she didn't care. She was quite prepared to endure anything that was done to her, and when the time came she would tell the whole world what she did.

'She said, "I asked Claude if he was engaged, and he told me, 'Not yet, but I hope to be', and it was then that I made up my mind that no one else should have him,"' Nellie went on. 'She also said, "I hope I will work my own salvation on earth and afterwards go to him, as I still owe him."

'Later I asked her where she had pawned her brooch to buy the revolver, and she said, "At the Mont de Piété in Castlereagh Street"—and afterwards she tore up the ticket, she told me.

'"You must have had a great nerve to do it," I said.

'"I did have a nerve," she answered. "When he came into the room, my heart failed me. I thought I could not do it, he looked so lovely. But after a time, when we were sitting on the sofa in the drawing room, I stood up to get a little present I had for him."

Nellie consulted her notes.

'She went on, "I held it in front of him, saying 'Here's my Christmas present to you, my darling,' and while he was looking at it and smiling, I took my revolver from the back of my dress with my right hand, and with my left hand around his neck, I shot him in the back of the head. Then I shot him in the side of the head, and then I walked round to the front of the couch and shot him again through his heart. Then I buttoned up his coat and waistcoat again. I knew for a certainty that every shot was fatal."

'Then she said, "I sat down and wrote some letters, and took two doses of laudanum. After that I felt for my heart, and where I felt it beating, I put the revolver to it and pulled the trigger. I lay in his arms and did not remember anything for two hours. When I came to, it was hard to get away from him, his arms were so stiff. I put the revolver in his lap. Then I locked him in the drawing room and went to my bedroom. Then my lady help came in and put me to bed. I knew I was dead then, because I heard them making a coffin for me outside."

'She was getting excited,' finished Nellie, 'and so I told her to calm down and not to worry. She appeared to be rational, and kept on repeating all this for days.'

In answer to Mr Mack, Nellie said that she could not remember exactly when she had first told anyone else about Mrs Mort's statements to her. It was some time after she had escorted her to the Penitentiary on 6 or 7 January, she thought.

'You can take it from me it was on January 11,' Mr Mack told her. 'And yet you made no notes at the time?'

'No.'

'And gave no evidence at the Coroner's Inquest?'
'No.'
'Humph!' said Mr Mack, and sat back down.

※

The prosecution's case ended with the reading of Harold Mort's deposition, and Dr Erasmus Bligh took the stand for the defence. He had known Dorothy since she was a schoolgirl in North Sydney about sixteen years ago, he told the court, and was about to repeat the opinion of one of her schoolmistresses of her when Mr Mack again raised an objection to his own witness. Being hearsay no doubt, this was upheld.

While he was familiar with Dorothy's earlier history, continued Dr Bligh, he had not encountered her again in 1913 when he had helped to treat her mother and brother after Mackay Woodruff's attack on their lives: 'I administered anaesthetics to them both,' he said, 'while the father was in the North Shore Hospital with his throat cut.' As a consultant at the same hospital he had visited Dorothy on 23 December, two days after Dr Tozer's death. At that date her chest had blood in it, she was feverish and showed signs of pneumonia, and he had felt that both her mental and physical condition were critical.

'In my opinion she was insane,' Bligh went on. 'I wanted to send her to Callan Park or Gladesville, where she would be under closer observation. I thought she was not safe where she was, and I asked for a female police attendant to watch over her, as we were afraid she might make another attempt on her own life.'

After consulting Drs Buckley and Palmer, he had

isolated her from the other patients, but he remained very dissatisfied with her state, and had the greatest difficulty in inducing her to sleep. To questions from Sidney Mack, Dr Bligh recounted that it was because of her elation at what had occurred, and her irrational statements, that Mrs Mort had struck him as being insane.

'Assuming that she shot Dr Tozer, did she know she'd done wrong?' asked Mr Mack.

'No. She seemed quite elated about it,' repeated Dr Bligh. 'Afterwards she rambled on, saying that after the shooting she had been taken away somewhere, she was not sure where. She told me that she was pregnant, and that Dr Tozer was the father. She also said that efforts had been made to remove the child from her; she was not clear how, but now that she was here at the hospital, she felt much happier, and she knew she would be looked after. Because Dr Tozer was dead, she said, she was going to marry his brother, and in that way when a grandson was born, Mrs Tozer and all the family would be pleased.'

'Of course, Dr Tozer had no brother?' asked Mr Mack.

'Yes, I knew that,' said Dr Bligh. 'Then she said she would like to leave, as she was going on a trip around the world and wanted to get her clothes ready. At the same time, she seemed elated about her own death, which she thought would occur shortly, and because her husband had built her a beautiful little coffin at home. She dilated upon it as any insane person might have done.'

'Did you form any opinion as to whether this was a pretence?' asked the Chief Justice.

In his opinion it was not, replied Dr Bligh. The form of insanity that Mrs Mort suffered from—emotional insanity—would be aggravated by any love excitement, and a disappointment in love would only aggravate it further.

'A neurotic woman, with an hereditary taint, who had it suddenly revealed to her that her lover was about to marry someone else, would she not be very likely to go insane?' asked Mr Mack.

'It would contribute to a fit of insanity,' Dr Bligh said. Her condition on December 23, he believed, was consistent with her having been insane for some time, and having examined her daily for some weeks after that, he hadn't changed his mind. Despite the insanity, he told Mr Mack, she might have been able then to give a clear account of the preceding events, but still be unable to give an account of them now.

'Could not Mrs Mort's condition after the tragedy also be consistent with that of a woman who had shot her lover and then realised the horror of it?' asked Mr Coyle.

Dr Bligh thought not.

'But you do agree that the killing of her lover alone does not mean that she was insane?' asked Mr Coyle.

'Yes,' said Dr Bligh. 'But then there was her elation afterwards. The act itself is not insane, but the elation is. And if, having killed the person she loved, she then determined to kill herself, and fired at herself while sitting on his knee with her arms around him, that, I think—the embracing of a dead body—is again a sign of insanity.'

'Might not the shock of the shooting and the taking of laudanum together account for it?' Mr Coyle asked.

'No, I do not think so,' repeated Dr Bligh.

'And yet if she were insane on the day of the tragedy, you would still expect her to be able to give a detailed account, days afterwards, of everything she did?'

'Yes, she might do that, and yet still be unbalanced in other respects,' said Dr Bligh. 'The shock of the tragedy might restore her sanity temporarily. For a person to commit an act that is obviously insane, and then become quite sane again after, is not uncommon.'

'A woman who had the wit to conceal her association with her lover from her husband for six months, and then find he was to marry someone else, and then kill him, could give a detailed account of what she did because the shock rendered her temporarily sane?' asked Mr Coyle.

'Yes,' said Dr Bligh.

Mr Coyle tried again. 'Would not the fact of her concealing her lover's existence from her husband also be consistent with sanity?'

'It might equally be consistent with insanity,' replied Dr Bligh. 'I would say her condition before the tragedy was quite consistent with insanity, but one could not be entirely definite, except to say that she was apparently a very ill woman.'

Hospital Superintendent Dr Emma Buckley, plump-faced and middle-aged; with blunt, capable hands and reddened knuckles, wore a monocle attached to her dress with a thin black cord. When she had known Dorothy as a girl she had been very emotional and highly-strung, she told the court, and as she grew older, Dr Buckley believed, these tendencies were likely to increase, especially in times of nervous strain.

When Mrs Mort was admitted into her care at the North Shore Hospital, continued Dr Buckley, she had been quiet, except to say repeatedly that she wouldn't make a statement. When asked if she knew where she was, Dorothy had thought at first she was in her parents' flat in Chatswood: she thought she could hear the voices of her husband and children outside the door, and wanted them brought in. As with the other doctors, Dorothy had told her that she wanted to marry Claude Tozer's brother, and would travel the world with him. This would please Mrs Tozer, she was convinced, as it would give her child his proper name, and then she would give the child to her.

'The reason she wanted to go for a trip around the world was so that the baby would be born in another country with no scandal attached,' explained Dr Buckley. 'She said to me, "You're coming too". Later she said, "We're not going away after all, because I am dead".'

'Bearing in mind the facts of the case, the hereditary taint in her blood, and her neurotic temperament, would you say that a calamity in love would be likely to unhinge her brain?' asked Mr Mack.

Dr Buckley agreed. 'Speaking from hearsay, the fact that there was another man in the case twelve months before would point to a tendency for that particular insanity of mind to run to the opposite sex,' she went on, seemingly unaware of the startling aspect of this new evidence. 'She often told me, as between one woman and another, of the various conquests she had made. She spoke of an aunt, or great aunt, who was very like her in physique, and remarked that she held the same attraction for men.

'Seeing her night and day at three-hourly intervals, I think I heard rather more of these matters than she might perhaps speak of to a man,' said Dr Buckley. 'The fact that she had received this disappointment; that for a time there had been an arrangement that she was to get a divorce and marry Tozer, and then suddenly he came to her and said he was going to marry someone else—I think all that would be sufficient to send her particular type of mind insane.'

Dr Buckley did not claim that any woman who would kill a man must be insane, she told Mr Coyle. 'But for a woman to shoot a man in the head, and then open up his waistcoat and shoot him through the heart, then button his waistcoat afterwards and lie in his arms in the way alleged, all this would indicate insanity to me. I don't think any woman in her right mind could sit in a dead man's lap for several hours after killing him.

'Any normal woman might kill a man, and any normal man might kill a woman, with provocation. But in the case of a married woman, with children, I do not think that a mere disappointment in love would cause her to kill. She has more at stake; she would have more caution about her—she has her children to take into account. In this case—the case of a married woman with children—I would say she was not normal. For a single woman, the circumstances might be different.'

'Do you think Mrs Mort knew what she was doing?' asked Mr Coyle.

'I think she knew she was shooting a man, and I

think she knew who he was,' replied Dr Buckley. 'But I don't know she knew it was wrong. I don't think she was capable of judging the gravity of the situation. She did not know the nature of the charge against her, I'm convinced of that.

'If she said she was determined that no other woman should have him, I don't think that proves anything either way. If a woman said that, or wrote it, it would indicate jealousy. But any woman might make a statement like that without intending to carry it out, so I don't think it would necessarily show purpose.'

NINETEEN

The Trial: the Second Day

On the morning of 8 April, the second day of the trial, there was a flutter in the public gallery as Mr Mack called a surprise witness.

Arthur Shirley—tall, slim, dark-haired, with matinee-idol good looks and striking blue eyes—had recently returned from America to set up a motion picture company, he told the court. In mid-September 1920, Dorothy Mort had called on him to ask if he would give her some work in his new film. He was not quite ready to begin production yet, he had said, but eventually agreed, telling her to come to his Rose Bay studio at 8.30 one morning in late November or early December.

During this first interview, Mrs Mort had struck him as not quite rational. On the two or three occasions he saw her afterwards, perhaps of twenty minutes each, she was depressed and anxious, and her condition seemed only to get worse. She told him that because of a great sorrow she had, her life was not worth living, but she believed that entering the motion picture business might help her to forget her troubles.

Despite saying she could not get there so early because of her sleepless nights, she had nevertheless arrived on the appointed day, very late. Seeming nervous and excited, she told him that two men had followed her on the footboard of the tram all the way from her home to the studio door.

Mr Shirley had thought at first it was possible that someone *had* followed her, and so went outside the studio with her, where Dorothy had pointed to a seat near the entrance and said, 'They are sitting over there.' When he'd told her no one was there, she'd answered, 'There is, I'm positive. They're talking about me now.' When he had asked her what were they were saying, she said, 'They're saying they're going to kill me.'

'I assured her that no one was there, and sent her upstairs to get ready, and made sure myself there were no strangers about,' Shirley said. 'Upstairs, she told all the other girls about the men. We motored out to the location and went on with the day's filming, but she was in great distress and very nervous. She wouldn't eat. She couldn't concentrate, and constantly I had to tell her what to do. She had no spirit or initiative, and she spoke of suicide. When I remonstrated with her, saying that life was sweet, she said she'd been so unhappy of late she had no desire to live.'

'Did she talk connectedly?' asked Mr Mack.

'No. She would wander from one subject to another, and couldn't carry on a normal conversation at all,' Mr Shirley said. 'She talked about herself, and her hats, and all day she maintained that there were strange men around the place. At the end of the day she was still certain that the two men had followed her on the tram.'

After the day's work, continued Mr Shirley, she said she wouldn't go back to the studio unless he accompanied her.

'I sent her back in the car with the other girls. At the studio, when the others had gone, she was still very frightened, saying that she had seen the men again on the running board of the car. But I was in the car behind them, and there was no one there. I urged her not to think about it, and tried to encourage her by telling her I wanted her in the picture. She said that in a few days she would be dead. At last I got her quiet, and I went with her to the tram and sent her home, and I haven't seen her since.'

When this witness had stepped down, William Coyle exercised his right to call additional evidence in reply, and Dr Robert Lee-Brown, the medical officer at Long Bay, was recalled. Mrs Mort had been under his observation daily at the gaol since January 7, for some three months, he told Coyle, and he had seen no trace of insanity in her.

'I suppose it would be quite possible for there to have been distinct signs of insanity before she arrived there, and yet to show no signs of it while at the Penitentiary?' asked the Chief Justice.

Sidney Mack objected to this, and Sir William Cullen—remarking that he thought the question went in Mr Mack's favour—said he would not press for an answer.

While he admitted that others had reported to him meaningless statements she had made, Dr Lee-Brown maintained in response to Mr Mack, he had heard none of them himself.

Sidney Mack rose and pointed dramatically towards the dock. Today, on the second day of her trial, Dorothy no longer wore her veil, so that the jurymen—although not the public—could see her face.

'There is the woman you are being asked to try for murder,' said Mr Mack. 'Look at what a wreck she is! If your verdict is one of guilty, then this poor wreckage of humanity will be sentenced to hang by her neck until she is dead. That is what a verdict of guilty will mean, Gentlemen, and that is what will happen. After all the anxiety, all the shame, all the untold horror she has suffered; after seduction and betrayal by the man she sacrificed everything for, you are asked to find her guilty of murder.'

He paused. The notion that even if Dorothy were found guilty, she was in little danger of being hanged, was not one that Mr Mack was likely to dwell on in a final address. Of the 256 men and 54 women charged with murder in New South Wales in the previous twenty years, only a dozen of the females had been convicted. Since 1899, when Louisa Collins was hanged for the poisoning of two of her husbands with arsenic, no woman in the state had been executed—although in other Australian states they were not quite so safe. Neither—in NSW or elsewhere—were men.

'And whom is she guilty of murdering?' asked Mr Mack.

'—He who was first her lover, and then her seducer, and finally her betrayer: a man who has betrayed not only her, but also the best and most sacred traditions of his noble profession. A profession that we all must trust—with our lives, with our wives, with our young girls and our little children.

'Look at her carefully,' Mr Mack instructed the jurors again. 'You are looking at a woman who has been through hell, and who is going through hell now. I put it to you—and I am not trying to arouse your sympathy—that she is here through the malpractice of a man who was trusted by her, and trusted by her husband!'

To claim a conviction, Mr Mack told them, the Crown must satisfy the jury beyond doubt that Dorothy Mort was guilty. It was not a question of possibility, or of probability: they must be satisfied that her conduct was consistent with guilt, and with no other theory than guilt. But even if they reached the conclusion that she had killed Dr Tozer, he went on, when the doctor died—and whether or not he died at her hand—Dorothy Mort was insane. The Crown witnesses themselves had said so!

'First you must find that she did this thing at all—but then, whether she did or not, she was absolutely mad!' he repeated. A victim of unspeakable sorrow for many years, Mrs Mort had gone through suffering enough to turn the brain of a hard-headed man—and she a fragile and weak woman!

'—An educated, a refined woman; but a sensitive one, and nervous—can you not imagine the awful effect on her of the tragedy involving her father? Wouldn't it rather be a matter for surprise if she were *not* mad?' Mr Mack asked. Her own father had committed suicide; *he* was indubitably insane, and the medical men had said themselves that his madness was in all probability transmitted. Was it any wonder that the daughter of a madman, under such strain, would go mad?

'The treatment for a woman such as this, the medical men had all agreed, was not to excite her or to play on her emotions,' continued Mr Mack. 'But what had Dr Tozer done? Called upon to treat her neurasthenia—the result of this very tragedy!—what did he do? Instead of healing her—instead of giving her soothing drugs—his actions were calculated to kill her. He *knew* that he should have tried to keep her calm, but instead he had administered a poison—not a material poison, but a mental one.

'This would-be gallant cavalier, before he had known her a fortnight, was telling her—his client's wife!—that they should "mingle their tears and sympathy together",' said Mr Mack. 'He talked of how she spent her dreary nights, as only a lover would dream of writing to a woman. And this from a doctor to his patient! He must have known how such intimate letters might tap into her emotions. It was a path that could lead only to madness!'

Mr Mack stepped closer to the jury box. 'I put it to you, Gentlemen, this doctor *knew* what sort of woman she was. He was not a layman. Was he thinking of her own good, or only his own selfish lust and pleasure? And then, by the end of August, he writes to her again, wondering how their situation is going to end. Apparently he has a gleam of conscience!'

Mr Mack leaned forward. '—And yet his only conclusion is that they should "gather happiness while they may".'

Mr Mack gazed at the twelve men arrayed in front

of him. 'Dr Tozer *knew* they were drifting towards danger, and yet he did nothing to help. He writes to her that in everyone there is a deep-seated fountain of emotion. He knows that of himself. Why, then, does he not keep away?

'No, instead he keeps on writing all this muck—this *poisonous* muck!—to her. And probably all the while he is thinking to himself what fine letters they are!

'Everything that made life worth living she would give up for him: her children, home, husband. Everything that she held dear, her honour included, she would sacrifice. The idea that she would eventually marry the doctor was the idea that had kept her sane—could they imagine her state when this was taken away?

'*Think* what these letters might have meant to this woman. Here you have a woman living in hope that she will marry her lover. It has been arranged that the whole matter should come out in the open, but it doesn't. Does the good doctor want to have anything to do with the divorce court? No, that would spoil his fine reputation! *He* was going to have his fun at her expense, and then ride away!'

Mrs Mort's confessions—her *alleged* confessions!—were made at a time when she was mad, he said. Would any sane woman chatter of these things to any and everyone? Were not the confessions themselves the strongest corroboration of the medical men's evidence? If the gentlemen of the jury concluded this, they must disregard everything she had said—or allegedly said. Well might the Crown pick out parts out of these statements and say—well, this bit is true, but this is not. If it were true that Mrs Mort had shot

Dr Tozer, then why was it not also true that she was pregnant to him? Without these confessions (which, of course, they must disregard because she was mad) the Crown had circumstantial evidence only, and this was insufficient to convict her. In no circumstances, therefore, could they safely bring a verdict of guilty.

Mr Mack then changed tack. Before they could find that Mrs Mort had killed Dr Tozer, he said, they must exclude every other possibility. From the evidence of her letter to Mrs Tozer, Dorothy had loved the doctor, and was even prepared to die for him. There was no hostility there; no sign of murderousness. In all of her letters, she wrote of planning to take only her own life. The night before the events, he reminded the jurors, she had a conversation with her husband.

'It was a long conversation. We do not know what it was about. We don't even know that the doctor's name was mentioned. But isn't it possible that she told her husband about the whole thing? Isn't it possible that she confessed to her double life, and that her husband then sent for the doctor to arrange for their future? Dr Tozer would see at once that he was ruined.

'Now, follow the likely subsequent events. Dr Tozer was called in next day to see Mrs Mort, and he went. What happened then, no one knows. But if Mrs Mort *had* told her husband everything, might she not then produce a revolver and shoot herself?

'And then what might Dr Tozer's reaction be? What state of panic would *he* be in?

'Professionally, he would be dead, faced with the certainty of the scandal of his relations with a married woman being revealed. Would not that play upon his mind? And then, Gentlemen, was Dr Tozer quite normal himself? What with the wound made to his brain made while defending his country (which is indeed to his credit), might not the shock have affected *his* brain?

'His honour was gone; the temptation was in front of him. The revolver was there. Wouldn't it be natural for the doctor to take up the weapon and shoot himself?

'Gentlemen, although the man is dead, I cannot spare him. He intended to seduce this woman, and he did not care!'

Mr Mack paused, and turned impressively to face the jury again. 'Why did God make these neurotic women?' he asked softly. 'The question might rather be,' he thundered, 'why did the Devil make these unworthy men?'

Sidney Mack's closing address to the jury had lasted an hour and a half. By the end of it, reported the *Sydney Morning Herald*, the Defence had amply demonstrated that it was possible for Dr Tozer—realising he had betrayed both Mrs Mort and his own profession—to have shot himself in the back of the head. Medical evidence had shown that it was possible for a man thus shot not to die immediately. Mr Mack had required the jury, if they were to find her guilty, to be absolutely certain that Mrs Mort had committed the murder.

William Coyle, for the Crown, began his closing address at 11.45 a.m. This lasted little more than fifteen minutes.

The Defence had thought fit to attack the memory and reputation of Dr Tozer, which he had a right to do, Mr Coyle told the jurors—but, he reiterated, they must remember that any test applied to the man must also apply to the woman, and both Mrs Mort and Dr Tozer had loved not wisely, but too well. Much as the doctor might have been at fault in his betrayal of Mrs Mort and his own honour, yet he had been prepared to marry her—it was Mrs Mort who would not finally agree to it, because of her children. Was he, then, the only one to be blamed?

'It is not always the woman who is seduced, sometimes it is the man,' Mr Coyle continued. 'There is nothing that can be said against one that cannot be said against the other. As Kipling has written, *"The sin that they do by two and two, they must pay for one by one."*

'And Dr Tozer has paid. Hot-blooded, he acted not wisely, and now he has paid.

'It is not always the woman who is seduced,' repeated Mr Coyle. 'Sometimes it is also the man, by the woman—and now the accused is before you to answer for her part.'

Now the jury must dry up any hot-blooded sympathy that ran naturally in their veins and turn themselves into calculating machines, and as such they must calculate the facts. The Defence had suggested that someone else might have shot Dr Tozer—but when Mr Palmer was in the witness stand, Mr Mack had not asked him a single question to support that proposition.

As for the idea that Dr Tozer had shot himself—would any medical man, in turning a weapon on himself, miss his own heart, and then, from an almost impossible position, try to shoot himself in the back of the head? And how, if Mrs Mort were shot first, could she then go on to list in such detail the wounds made afterwards to Dr Tozer?

The purchase of the revolver, and—after the event—the tearing-up of the card and photograph, the buttoning up of the waistcoat, pointed clearly to who had fired the shots. Mrs Mort had committed the crime, and had admitted it. Regarding the plea of insanity, whatever her condition before or after, there was no evidence that Mrs Mort had been insane on the day of the tragedy. Later, she could well have been unbalanced by shock. No doubt she could easily be pushed over the edge, but the shock that *might* have unhinged her—of Dr Tozer telling her of his intent to marry another—had occurred days before. Was she unhinged when she wrote to Mrs Tozer? All her actions from that time on, as well as her accounts of them afterward, were those of a sane person.

The probabilities were that Dorothy Mort, having shot Dr Tozer, had then shot herself, resolving that they should die together in a way which—fortunately—one seldom saw today except in the moving pictures. Normal or abnormal, she had acted on the primitive theory that, loving a man and being unable to have him, no other woman should. Instead they would perish together, and their beautiful love would go on forever. It might be a mad woman's theory—but might it not be also the theory of a sane woman?

'You are aware of the facts, Gentlemen,' finished Mr Coyle. 'It is for you to decide whether this woman is guilty or innocent; sane or insane. The responsibility is yours; thank heaven it is not mine. We know you will do your duty. If you find that she is insane, then your duty will be a pleasant one. If you have any reasonable doubt as to her sanity, then again it will be pleasant. But if, on the whole of the facts, you are satisfied that Mrs Mort knew what she was doing—then, Gentlemen, it is your painful duty to return a verdict, in accordance with the evidence, of guilty.'

The prosecutor William Coyle, so as not to alienate the male jurors by appearing to attack an ill and vulnerable woman, had largely refrained from blackening Dorothy's character. Instead he concentrated on establishing that, whatever her condition before or after, she was sane at the moment of Claude's death.

Sidney Mack's argument, on the other hand, had been two-pronged: firstly, Dorothy had indeed been insane at that moment, and secondly—rather more of a long shot—that the jury could not be entirely sure who had shot Dr Tozer anyway. Most of his time, however, was spent in a histrionic effort to portray Claude Tozer as an old-fashioned bounder and cad, with Dorothy his pitiful victim whom no gentlemanly juror could convict. His tactics were sufficiently confusing that some believed, according to one press account, he was arguing that Claude had shot not only himself, but Dorothy as well.

Dorothy was not called to the witness box. Sidney Mack would have recognised immediately the dangers of exposing her to William Coyle's formidable cross-examination skills. Nor, given her propensity to confess, would he allow her to make a statement from the dock, as was her right. If Dorothy had hoped to use her trial as a platform from which to explain her actions, then either her health or her counsel's tactics thwarted her. The jury was exposed to the sight of either a very frail and ill (or perhaps heavily sedated) woman, or a premeditated display at Mack's behest to enlist the court's sympathy—Dorothy's last public theatrical performance.

Sir William Cullen began his summation at ten past twelve and finished twenty-five minutes later. He cautioned the jury not to be swayed by any appeal to sentiment, but to try the case on the facts alone. Their only question was whether the Crown had made its case beyond reasonable doubt.

The Defence had advanced the theory that Dr Tozer had committed suicide, he told the jurors—but Dr Palmer had said he did not think all three wounds could be self-inflicted, and here the medical evidence would guide them. They must also consider how far Dr Tozer's war injuries might have affected his conduct.

On the question of insanity, Sir William went on, they must consider whether the accused knew the nature of her acts, and could see the difference between right and wrong. They must judge her condition in the light of previous and subsequent events. They must take into account the insanity of her father, who had exhibited murderous tendencies himself. Two medical men had been called by the Crown, and two by the Defence, and they must weigh their respective opinions. Again, the medical evidence would guide them on whether the accused's statements or confessions could be relied upon. If the jury held that Mrs Mort was insane, Sir William concluded, then she was not punishable.

At 12.35 p.m. the jury filed out to consider their verdict.

The day's proceedings so far had taken little more than two and a half hours. During the summing up, Dorothy—still seated behind her screen—appeared to have fallen asleep on her attendant's shoulder, and remained so when the jury retired. Now, when asked to walk into an anteroom, reported a newspaper, she fell back in her chair, deathly white, and seemed to swoon. When smelling salts failed to rouse her, two constables carried her out in the chair in which she sat—at which point all the women in the public gallery stood up and craned their necks to see her.

'It was noticeable,' observed the *Daily Telegraph*, 'that the men in the audience were not so curious.'

TWENTY

The Verdict

At 2.25 p.m., after lunching in the jury room, the jurors signalled that they were ready to return. Dorothy, who evidently had recovered from her fainting fit in the intervening two hours, walked back into the courtroom unaided, with the gaol matron following behind. In the packed stalls, the female spectators again all rose in a body and gaped. But before Mrs Mort had been seated more than a few minutes, the press observed, she appeared to swoon again and had to be supported on both sides. The jurors re-entered at 2.30 p.m. precisely. Invited to deliver their verdict, the foreman stood and announced firmly, 'Guilty whilst of unsound mind.'

There was a startled silence, a murmur, and then the Chief Justice intervened. 'I take it your verdict, then, is not guilty on the ground of insanity?'

Looking confused, the foreman repeated, 'Our verdict is guilty whilst of unsound mind.'

Sir William appeared perturbed. In an Australian court, as both Mr Coyle and Mr Mack well knew, Dorothy Mort could either be insane or guilty, but not both.

'Under our law, where you are satisfied the accused is insane at the time of the commission of the act, the correct verdict is "not guilty on the ground of insanity",' the Chief Justice instructed the jurors. 'If you have a talk with other members of the jury, I have no doubt that you will all agree with that.'

The foreman looked at his fellows, and replied, 'Your Honour, we have agreed on that.' Several other jurors nodded in assent.

'The woman is, therefore, acquitted on the ground of insanity?' asked Mr Coyle.

'It may be otherwise in other countries, but I have never known a verdict in these circumstances to be returned in any other words,' said Sir William. In delivering his judgment, he directed that under the conditions of the *Lunacy Act* of 1898, Dorothy Mort should be held in the State Reformatory for Women until the Governor's Pleasure was known.

Dorothy, still in a swoon, was carried out in her chair. Inside a spiked gate giving onto a dank and narrow lane at the rear of the Court building, a car was once again waiting to take her back to Long Bay.

We all have our dreams. Without them we should be clods. It is in our dreams that we accomplish the impossible; the rich man dumps his load of responsibility and lives in a log shack on a mountaintop, the poor man becomes rich, the stay-at-home travels, the wanderer finds an abiding place.

—Ralph Stock, *The Cruise of the Dream Ship*,
London 1921

Part Three

The Aftermath

TWENTY-ONE

Dorothy Alone

On 7 January 1921 they helped her to dress and drove her from the North Shore Hospital to the vehicle punt on the harbour, and then on through the city and down Oxford Street by the old sandstone Darlinghurst Court House. From the motorcar window she saw the grassy paddock of Randwick racecourse as they travelled along Bunnerong Road beside the long, straight tram tracks that led out through the flat southern suburbs. Scatterings of small weatherboard houses gave way to an impoverished coastal strip of swamp and stunted bush.

Eight miles from the city they passed a cluster of ramshackle wooden cottages where groups of squatting Aborigines in ragged clothing looked up expressionlessly as the motorcar went by. Then came the fishing boats of La Perouse and the Coast Hospital, its old stone Lazaret rising grimly against a backdrop of windswept sandy waste and flat grey sea echoing with the cry of gulls. Beside the road she might have seen a work gang of male prisoners in white canvas trousers, grey jackets and floppy cabbage tree hats shamble sullenly along, heads down in single file, while a uniformed man on horseback, draped in a cartridge belt and holding a carbine, kept guard. Driving past a line of high walls and forbidding watchtowers they finally reached an ornate brick gatehouse.

Inside the brick arch, women in crisp blue cotton uniforms took down Dorothy's particulars in a large ledger and told her what they wanted her to do. In a small, grey room she removed her skirt and blouse and submitted while they lifted her hair and patted and parted her legs, before taking away her clothes and leading her into a second room, where she was measured and weighed. They told her to shower, and then dress in the pile of coarse garments they had placed in her arms.

TWENTY-TWO

Mad or Bad?

p 585 *Hysteria*: ... Hysteria occurs most frequently between the ages of 15 and 25. The most common causes are sexual excesses, novel-reading, perverted habits of thought, idleness and some forms of ovarian or uterine disease. It occurs most frequently among young ladies who have been reared in luxury and who have never learnt self-control ... The affection is not, as many people suppose, wholly an imaginary disease, but is really a malady of considerable gravity.

Page 589: *Neurasthenia* ... (exhaustion of the nervous system): Constant overwork or worry, too much excitement, too little physical exercise or recreation ... [may] result in imperfect nutrition of the nerve centres, and then follows any number of and variety of secondary disturbances ... the gynecologist is too likely to look no further than the womb and ovaries; and the general practitioner is apt to imagine spinal disease, dyspepsia, "liver complaint," or "malaria" to be at the bottom of the trouble. The patient, not her disease or diseases, should be made the object of treatment.

—*Ladies' Guide in Health and Disease*,
by J.H. Kellogg, M.D., London

In Claude Tozer's time, the study of madness was still in its infancy at Sydney University's Medical Faculty. An introductory course in psychological medicine under Dr J. Froude Flashman or Andrew Davidson was offered, while Professor Francis Anderson lectured in mental and moral sciences in the Department of Philosophy. Little had changed since the previous century, and despite his obvious medical skills, Claude was as ill-equipped as any to help Dorothy Mort.

In the cases of women in particular, definitions of illness sometimes overlapped with qualitative assessments involving morality and vice. Custodianship of the insane in Australia had developed out of the colonial convict system, when the Governor was able to order anyone he considered a danger to the community to be restrained. By 1843, to prevent abuses of this power, the *Dangerous Lunatics Act* required that two medical practitioners certify such persons before they were committed to an asylum.

Although the 1843 Act offered some protection against wrongful detention, a 'lunatic' was nevertheless defined as anyone 'idiot, lunatic or of unsound mind or incapable of managing himself or his affairs': a broad sweep that included habitual drunks, the retarded or senile, and in some cases, epileptics. Besides demonstrating a 'derangement of mind', any person manifesting an intent to commit suicide (or other criminal act) could be forcibly examined by doctors or magistrates for signs of lunacy, as—for their own safety—could those found 'wandering at large' or being cruelly treated by family or employers. Well into the twentieth century, women showing symptoms of 'moral imbecility'—usually promiscuity or unfaithfulness, or some other inability or unwillingness to be bound by prevailing sexual mores—could also be certified as mad. Men exhibiting similar symptoms were not considered to suffer from the same affliction.

Further legislation in 1878 provided for the regular medical inspection of lunatics and the safeguarding of their property. The *Lunacy Act* of 1898 went on to differentiate between the criminally and non-criminally insane. The section pertaining to Dorothy's sentencing—paragraph three of Section 65 of Part Five—specified that a person found to be insane while committing a crime should be confined in a gaol or certified hospital, as the Governor saw fit. However, by the early 1900s, local asylums such as Gladesville and Callan Park were so overcrowded that Dorothy had little chance of being sent to one.

Mental illnesses were largely thought to arise from underlying biological conditions, some of which were exclusive to—or, in the case of hysteria, almost inherent in—women, who were believed to be especially prone to such disorders because of their sexual and reproductive physiology. Early in the nineteenth century the influential physician James C. Prichard, a Commissioner of Lunacy in London, had posited that inherited insanity could often lie dormant until triggered by external events, and just as rapidly abate. Alienists also believed that brooding on the likelihood of such a degrading hereditary complaint could bring madness on.

With such current beliefs about the heritability of these tendencies (particularly from mother to daughter), mental illness in a Victorian family was a cause for deep shame—and the daughters of such families often became unmarriageable, if the 'taint' became widely bruited about.

Public perceptions of female lunacy were also influenced by popular writers such as Charles Dickens and Wilkie Collins, the forerunners of modern detective novelists. Collins's sensational novel *The Woman in White* (1860) dealt in part with a woman falsely confined in a lunatic asylum, while his story 'Mad Monkton' (1855) concerned hereditary insanity. Other well-known examples included Charlotte Brontë's archetypal Mrs Rochester (1847), *Villette* in 1853, and Charlotte Perkins Gilman's chilling story 'The Yellow Wallpaper' (1892)—in such fictional devices, the imprisonment of women for insanity, false or otherwise, could often allow a man to re-partner or take unhindered possession of his wife's fortune. While male lunatics were often popularly portrayed as murderous maniacs, females were sometimes seen as equally threatening, but with the added undertone of sexual unease.

In reality, relatively few women of the period (sane or insane) committed murder. Infanticide did occur, but very few killed their consorts—and if they did, it was most often by less overtly violent means such as poisoning. Often these latter crimes were underpinned by motives that were easily understood: fear of a partner's violence against herself or her children; or greed—for monetary gain or inheritance; or to remove an obstacle to a new lover. In rarer cases, it was revenge: 'love to hatred turned'.

But why would any woman kill a man she loved? Was it likely that a desperate but sane woman would determine that she could not live without another, and then—while still in love with him—decide that he should accompany her in death? Or was Dorothy Mort a pitiable figure, sinking deeper and deeper into some form of mental breakdown in a way that was rightly recognised by the court?

A court artist's sketch from the time of the coronial inquest—one of only two images I could locate from the period before her imprisonment—showed her wearing a soft tunic jacket in a *faux* military style, with epaulettes and buttoned pockets, along with a jaunty AIF-style felt hat pinned up at one side: perhaps some fashionably patriotic gesture. Dorothy was always careful with the appropriateness of her costume. In this drawing, probably copied from an earlier press photograph now lost, she was once again portrayed with a dramatic dark rosebud mouth, her eyes wide and shaded with cross-hatching. Was there something always a little too measured in the way she presented herself? In pitying her, I had got her completely wrong?

'Think of her ornamental filigree handwriting, her Geisha makeup, her need to be "revered", her clever fingers making costumes,' a less sympathetic friend suggested.

Beatrice Tozer, too, had found Dorothy's manner 'studied'. Was she a cold fish, and so monstrously narcissistic that she could not admit rejection by a lover she wanted? Did she prefer to preserve the illusion (to herself and the world) that Claude still loved her, and to freeze the moment forever in the lie of a suicide pact, rather than face the reality that he had left her? If she had died as she planned, what the world would have seen was a Romeo and Juliet tableau, carefully stage-managed, with herself lying in Claude's dead arms. Was Dorothy so childish as to wish to close her eyes and pretend? To veil Claude's apparent treachery from others, as well as from herself? Surely such denial *would* make her, in modern clinical terms, insane?

And how guileless was she, with her womanly 'wiles' that had at first so amused Claude? Was she in fact more of a sexual predator than she appeared? There was further oddity here. Over the course of the trial, both the popular press and the prosecutor William Coyle had refrained from painting Dorothy as a scarlet woman, despite ample opportunity to do so. After a few sly hints at the illicit nature of her relationship with her doctor, even *Truth* had refrained from the stereotypes of seductress and adulterer, flouter of conventional morality, that such crimes normally attracted. Emma Buckley's evidence concerning an alleged previous lover or admirer was also mentioned briefly and then ignored by both sides.

By the time of her trial, the balance of professional opinion held that Dorothy Mort was insane: at the instant of Claude's death as well as before and after. Three out of the four medical men, her own husband and several other witnesses—even the newspapers—concurred on this. Florence Fizelle was also convinced—or wished to convey—that her mistress was insane. As time passed, Miss Fizelle's vague descriptions were replaced by more precise terms and her language became increasingly clinical. By 8 April, according to the trial transcript, instead of 'out of her mind' or 'like a wild woman', Florence was using phrases like 'in a demented condition'.

And if Dorothy was insane, she was innocent. As the Chief Justice had clearly explained in his summing up, Dorothy was not responsible for her act if she did not know what she was doing at the time, or otherwise could not judge that it was wrong.

Yet, to all appearances, Dorothy was perfectly aware all along of her actions, and also that they would be deemed wrong by the legal system, other people, and a higher power. Not long before the shooting she wrote to her mother asking God's forgiveness—although probably at this point only for the sin of taking her own life. She had 'never thought or meant to be wicked', she wrote. And the day after Claude's death she begged forgiveness of her victim's mother.

Dorothy also seemed to believe that she should expiate her crime on earth, while simultaneously welcoming her own death as a fitting end and consequence. In her later confessions—'they can do with me what they like'—she accepted she should be punished according to the law, although she evidently also believed that, together, Claude's death and her own would satisfy some higher scheme of things. Her attempts to confess were often thwarted by those who did not want her to incriminate herself. But although her actions were planned and premeditated over several days and stages, whether she could distinguish fantasy from reality is less clear.

※

While in her normal state of mind, Dorothy, like many women, had longed for a more glamorous life; when in a heightened state of illness or excitement, she was transparently a fantasist.

'Shall I make you care? Shall I make you love me?' asked 'The Sheik' of desert heroine Diana Mayo in Edith M. Hull's eponymous bestselling novel of the era. The book was available in Australia in early 1920, and a year later it became a successful feature film. Had Dorothy nurtured the idea that a desperate and theatrical act might solve her real-life problems, as it always seemed to do on stage or screen? After she had bought laudanum (using a ruse), sold an item of jewellery (using her stage name) and purchased a gun (for a fictional reason), was she merely acting out some highly melodramatic—even heroic—part in her own mind when she shot Claude Tozer and then tried to kill herself?

For Dorothy, however, there was no red velvet curtain to finally come sweeping down, either to permanent darkness, applause, or a return to ordinary life.

Nonetheless, despite her obvious mental stress, her apparently crazed and delusional ramblings, as described by several doctors, were somewhat less damning when seen from Emma Buckley's perspective. Her patient was considerably more forthcoming to her than to her male colleagues, as Buckley herself had remarked.

A pioneering female medical student at the University of Sydney, Dr Buckley had served as an AIF pathologist in London during World War I before returning to take up a research post especially created for her at Royal North Shore Hospital. On 23 December 1920, Dorothy's first day in her care, Dr Buckley recounted that her patient believed she was in 'her flat in Chatswood'—most probably Corona, where she had lived as a girl. If heavily medicated (or 'induced to sleep', as Dr Bligh had put it), Dorothy might well have been confused about where she was. Unfamiliar voices in the hospital corridors may well have reminded her of her children calling to her from outside the drawing room door while she lay in a drugged trance in her dead lover's arms.

Dorothy also believed—wishfully—that she was pregnant. Neither eating nor sleeping, wasted away now to just six stone, her menstruation had probably stopped. They had 'tried to take the baby away', she told the doctors—perhaps a befuddled memory of Dr Murray's attempts, in her bedroom at Ingelbrae, at siphoning her stomach contents with a rubber tube. Not wanting 'to have blood taken' reflected her fear of such an invasive treatment happening again.

Her projected trip around the world, Dr Buckley explained, was so that her baby might be born without a scandal. It was a not-uncommon ploy in Sydney society at the time for a respectable middle-class matron to take her erring daughter on a year-long 'European tour' (and subsequently to adopt out the baby) when just such an inconvenient circumstance arose. The cover story of being married to Claude's brother would give her son—and Dorothy assumed it would be a son—his correct name of Tozer. The child would compensate Beatrice for her loss, and she could be forgiven.

Then, in a deeper confusion, Dorothy again embraced the idea that she was already dead, but conscious of events in the mortal world she had left, as per 'Conan Doyle's spiritualistic theories'. She had heard her coffin being made outside, she said. Did this refer again to a memory of lying in an opium dream in the Ingelbrae drawing room while Florence and her children knocked repeatedly at the door from outside? Was this small coffin—white, and just two feet long—for the child she imagined had been taken from her surgically; or even for some other child lost previously to miscarriage or stillbirth? There had been rumours of a child dying, among the neighbours. Dorothy's reference in her letter to her mother to 'going across to the other side soon', indicate that she believed in a percipient afterlife.

Dorothy's apparent death wish is also explicable in light of earlier events. After her father's descent into insanity and eventual suicide, Dorothy had developed a morbid conviction that she had inherited a psychological taint. She believed that 'history would repeat itself'—she was doomed to go mad and possibly harm herself or her children. Her own death would certainly safeguard against this happening.

Her reaction—imagining her children were burning when she accidentally set her bed alight—also becomes more comprehensible with this hypothesis. Was her 'hysteria' merely a symptom of such an underlying fear? Was it her guilt at her own neglect of them—real or imagined—due to her affair with Claude, that drove these fears and conflicts? From the evidence extant, Dorothy was proud of her pretty daughter and much concerned by any health problems in her son—and yet she was prepared to leave them motherless through self-harm. In hindsight, her self-dramatising behaviour and repeated suicide threats (made to Florence, Harold and even relative strangers like Arthur Shirley), seem a cry for help.

Dr Buckley's unique perceptions of Dorothy's insanity were based on her beliefs about how a 'normal' woman would (or should) react to a failed love affair. While Dr Buckley—herself soon to marry a fellow doctor—agreed with her colleagues that Dorothy was of unsound mind, her more detailed explanations of Dorothy's thinking inadvertently undermined the allegations.

TWENTY-THREE

In Hindsight

A rush of tears blinded her and she stepped back uncertainly and stumbled against the little writing-table. She caught at it behind her to steady herself, and her fingers touched the revolver he had laid down. The contact of the cold metal sent a chill that seemed to strike her heart. She stood rigid, with startled eyes fixed on the motionless figure in the doorway—one hand gripping the weapon tightly and the other clutching the silken wrap across her breast. Her mind raced forward feverishly …

She closed her teeth on her trembling lip, her fingers tightened on the stock of the revolver, and a wild light came into her sad eyes. She could never go through with it. To what end would be the hideous torture? What was life without him?—Nothing and less than nothing. She could never give herself to another man …

Slowly she lifted the weapon clear of the table with steady fingers and brought her hand stealthily from behind her. She looked at it for a moment dispassionately. She was not afraid.
She was conscious only of an overwhelming weariness, a longing for rest that should still the gnawing pain in her breast

and the throbbing in her head … A flash and it would be over, and all her sorrow would melt away … But would it? A doubting fear of the hereafter rushed over her. What if suffering lived beyond the border-line? But the fear went as suddenly as it had come, for with it came remembrance that in that shadowy world she would find one who would understand—her own father, who had shot himself, mad with heartbroken despair …

She lifted the revolver to her temple resolutely.

—*The Sheik,* Edith M. Hull, 1919

At the time of the trial, the *Sydney Morning Herald* recorded Emma Buckley as saying that Dorothy Woodruff, as a schoolgirl, had been 'very emotional and hysterical'. However, this was not backed up by the trial transcript, which recorded only the words 'emotional and highly strung'. Nevertheless, Dr Buckley's is the earliest description we have of Dorothy's state of mind.

According to Harold Mort, who at first denied to police that his wife suffered from any mental illness at all, her first episode of instability—a 'nervous breakdown'—had occurred around September 1913, when Dorothy was twenty-eight, and it coincided with Mackay Woodruff's own descent into madness. The couple were still living in Woollahra, and Dorothy had had to 'bear the brunt' of her father's trial and the injuries he had inflicted on her mother and brother. This was also the year after the birth of her first child Poppy. Her son Pat's birth followed soon after in 1915, the year Mackay Woodruff was released from gaol.

A generation on, Mort descendants would ascribe Dorothy's 'trouble' to post-natal depression. In the period before that, a wall of silence had descended. Dorothy's children Poppy and Pat, a relative maintained, had grown to adulthood unaware of the events surrounding their mother's disappearance from their lives: all through her nine years in prison, they, along with their young Mort cousins, believed that she was merely away lying ill in a hospital somewhere.

When War was declared, despite belonging to the University Scouts, Harold Mort had stayed home rather than joining the Imperial Forces. A second breakdown had followed in 1917, he told the Coroner's Court, at around the time of their move to Cheltenham, when the children were five and two. Any such pre-existing disturbance was exacerbated when Dorothy's father killed himself in New Zealand in December 1919: it was from Christmas that year, Harold said, that he first noticed Dorothy's 'fits of depression', although at that time he did not consider her 'abnormal'.

In May 1920 the couple moved from Cheltenham to Lindfield. Ten years into her marriage, Dorothy found herself at thirty-five a suburban matron with two young children and an older husband who was frequently absent. From July that year, twice-weekly in the evenings, she journeyed by tram and ferry to Seaforth for acting lessons, further diminishing the couple's time together. In rehearsals, her teacher related, Dorothy was required to handle a toy gun on stage, and had offered to bring in her own pistol. Sidney Mack no doubt hoped that revealing this fact would help to explain Dorothy's purchase of a firearm.

A further secret first publicly revealed at the trial was that Dorothy's relationship with Dr Tozer was not the first love affair she had contemplated.

If this liaison had occurred, however, Harold gave no sign he knew of it and evidently it did not disrupt the marriage. Emma Buckley's surprising evidence—'that there was another man in the case twelve months before'—dates this attraction to late 1919. In December 1920 Dorothy told William Cowles the gunsmith that her husband was in India with Ralph Stock, and later told Beatrice Tozer of allegedly giving a pistol to 'a man going to Morocco'.

When Ralph Stock first visited Sydney in October 1910, he spent several months wandering the city, making connections with newspaper editors, artists and others in the literary world. Norman Lindsay, publisher of his first Australian stories, was a friend of Harold's sister Eirene Mort, who by then was writing and illustrating pieces for the *Sydney Mail*, which also printed a number of Stock's tales. As well, Stock wrote several plays. By the time he left Sydney for the second time in September 1914, Lillian Rock Phillips had moved to Seaforth.

By June 1920 Stock was back in Sydney again. In his dugout in France, he recorded, instead of a photograph of 'a fluffy girl' in his letter case, he had pored over plans for a vessel in which to sail for the South Seas. Invalided out of the army in September 1917, he headed for the Devon coast and within six months, through selling short stories and 'assiduously cultivating a maiden aunt', he accumulated enough capital to buy his *Dream Ship*, a 47-foot Norwegian pilot cutter. Several more months of night-trawling with the South Devon fishing fleet provided the funds to fit her out.

With £100 between them, Ralph, his sister Mabel and an ex-army officer friend, Steve Rundle, set sail. The *Dream Ship* carried them via Spain, the Canary Islands and Barbados to the Panama Canal, where they ran out of money. Around Christmas 1919, just as they were losing hope of continuing, Stock heard from his New York agent that a story of his had sold to United Artists for a sum that kept them going to the Galapagos Islands and Tahiti.

Then, in a bar in the Friendly Isles, according to his own account, Stock 'accidentally' sold the *Dream Ship* by naming to a buyer a price he thought too high for anyone to contemplate. Steve remained in Samoa, while Ralph and Mabel took a commercial liner, the *Makura*, to Australia, where he searched the coastal seaports for a replacement vessel before returning to Sydney. Towards the end of June 1920 the first chapter of 'The Voyage of the Dream Ship' appeared in the *Sydney Mail*.

Ralph Stock published several collections of stories over the next few years. Most were set in his Pacific ports-of-call, but a few touched on life in Sydney. One tale from the period, 'Pretenders', from *South of the Line* in 1922, features an actress who plays an unfaithful wife called 'Di'. 'The Test of Monaki', the work that had rescued the *Dream Ship*'s voyage from abandonment, appeared first in *Collier's Magazine* in New York in September 1919 as 'Black Beach', and then in a collection called *Beach Combings* the following May. It went through two more name changes—'The Gamest Girl' and 'The Girl who Dared'—before finally reaching the screen as *The Love Flower* in late 1920.

In a melodramatic low-budget feature directed by the legendary D.W. Griffith, a gimlet-eyed detective called Crane hires Sanders, the young master of a dilapidated copra trader, to help him hunt for a fugitive who—unjustly accused of murder—has fled with his loyal daughter Stella to a Pacific island. The pursuers eventually reach a remote atoll, Monaki, where a hidden sea passage leads them inside the crater to a secret lagoon. Here, beyond a black sand beach, a beautiful dark-haired girl watches their approach from a hut of reeds. When Stella—played by Carol Dempster—swims out and scuttles their cutter to prevent her father's capture, Sanders and Crane are forced to wait for rescue by a passing ship. Inevitably, Stella and Sanders fall in love, but cannot be together until Sanders finds a way to rid them of the detective who threatens their freedom. When *The Love Flower* was released in August 1920, it received mixed reviews.

In the meantime, by late June the same year, while Stock was revisiting Sydney after the *Dream Ship*'s voyage, Mrs Rock Phillips had moved her acting classes to Seaforth, near Stock's old haunts in Manly. By July, as well as rehearsing her leading part in 'Back Fire'—about a love triangle—Dorothy was also auditioning for a film role with Arthur Shirley. Stock—playwright, bit-part actor, and now motion picture author—was no doubt moving in the same circles.

When Claude Tozer had joined the Royal Australian Army Medical Corps in 1915, his earlier misanthropic habits hadn't changed. On 2 August 1916, a week after he was blown up at Pozières, Corporal Tom 'Rusty' Richards, a stretcher bearer with the First Field Ambulance, made a diary note of a conversation with his fellows: 'Strange, out of the three of them, they agreed that an act of providence must have directed the shell on top of so miserable a man as Tozer seems to be. They say he never would speak decently to anybody at all, and was a curse to work with.'

Another contemporary, Leonard May, an army doctor who had graduated with Claude from Sydney

University, recorded that Tozer had pipped him for the position of RMO to the 12th Battalion after the battle of Menin Road. Apparently, 'Aunty Tozer' had 'stronger pull in high places'. Len May referred to Claude in his wartime diary as 'that old frigidity', and yet repeatedly sought him out for games of piquet and chats, and volunteered to take his morning sick parades when Claude was ill. After mentioning him in passing more than a dozen times, May also recorded when Tozer received his DSO.

Following his injuries at Pozières, Claude's continuing headaches would not have improved his mood; however, his surly dedication (or inability to suffer fools) stood him in good stead. On his death, the *Bulletin* characterised him as 'the sort of M.O. every battalion wanted', with 'a wonderful ear for a hard luck story' and an ability to 'stand up to the most despotic of brass hats'. Having recovered and requested to be sent back to the front, he had pulled strings to be reunited with the men with whom he had left Gallipoli. Demobbed in May 1919, he moved in with Beatrice at Roseville and by June 1920—despite the lingering effects of his war wounds, two bouts of influenza, an attack of diphtheria and an operation for appendicitis—he was playing first class cricket again.

In the 1920s, Sydney was a closely interconnected city. Harold Mort's father Henry Wallace Mort and William Apedaile Charlton were both Canons of St Andrew's Cathedral. Claude's other clergyman uncle, Leopold Charlton, was Rector at St Martin's church at Killara, two stops up the railway line from Roseville. And so, despite the fact that James Murray, a senior physician with long experience in nervous disorders was living just around the corner in Tryon Road, it was young Dr Tozer, a mile away in Roseville, that Harold asked to treat his wife.

TWENTY-FOUR

The Love Flower

'For every girl that becomes ambitious for the stage, fifty now pine to go into the movies. The cheap and screaming publicity of the American companies, the intimate stories of artist's lives, the whirlwind rise of unknown girls to stardom, the eternal struggle for notoriety by the stars—these and a host of other things distract our young women's and young men's attention from their everyday business and make them dream of fame and fortune in the movies.'

—Beaumont Smith, *The Green Room,* March 1919

Like Lily Rock Phillips, the actor and film producer Arthur Shirley had travelled some distance from his origins by the time his path crossed with Dorothy's in the years immediately after World War I. Born in Hobart, he left school early and worked for Tattersall's lottery and as a solicitor's clerk before joining, at sixteen, an acting troupe that toured Tasmania in a two-horse caravan. After further stints at hawking groceries and in a Catholic seminary in Melbourne, he had returned to the stage in Sydney, where he built up a reputation as a knockabout actor, most famously for his appearance in Raymond Longford's pioneering film *The Silence of Dean Maitland* in 1914.

Soon after, Shirley had sabotaged his Australian career by suing a theatre manager and sailed for New York, where a small group of Australians had already breached the American studios. In 1916 he appeared with Louise Lovely in her American movie debut *Stronger than Death* and, as a sideline, started up a photography studio specialising in glamorous portraits of the stars. In June 1920, at thirty-four and with some twenty American screen credits behind him, he made a triumphal return to Sydney to set up his own film company, Shirley (Arthur) Productions Ltd.

With the slogan 'Moving Pictures Made in Australia for the World' and offices at 14 Martin Place, Shirley announced that he would bring the latest Hollywood movie-making techniques to his homeland. The company would construct a large Californian-style studio with film laboratories, sound stages and the latest lighting equipment. The local press, ever willing to welcome a returning hero, paid eager attention.

In the flurry of publicity that followed, Shirley told journalists that while homeward bound on the *Sonoma* he had met an American writer from the *Saturday Evening Post*, Pat O'Cotter, who had come up with a photoplay for his first feature. While 'written around Australian', *The Throwback* was a South Seas saga with a 'romantic plot, heart interest and gripping situations' that climaxed in Hawaii. An American star and crew were already signed up, so that the homegrown industry might benefit from their expertise until it found its feet.

Soon after, Shirley bought 'Ellerslie', a big

two-storey house at 336 New South Head Road in Rose Bay, and converted it to a temporary studio. By July 1920, *The Picture Show* magazine reported, Shirley was engaging the local 'types' he needed for the production, and hoped to have a cast assembled by the time the Americans arrived. The 'foreign' sequences would be shot at a mock Hawaiian village at Newport Beach, north of Sydney. But even at this early date Shirley's ambitious plans were beginning to unravel. Filming was repeatedly delayed while expensive alterations were made to the Rose Bay premises, and many scenes were shot in private houses.

According to Claude's first letter to Dorothy, it was in early July 1920—just as Shirley was looking for his local 'extras'—that Dorothy first auditioned for a film role. Claude wished her luck in beguiling the 'American' producer. If Arthur Shirley were already beset by financial difficulties, the flock of starry-eyed and eager amateurs crowding into local film academies such as that of Mrs Rock Phillips's presented an attractive proposition.

TWENTY-FIVE

Claude at Cricket

> For weeks past the young doctor's name has been on every cricket enthusiast's lips because of his possible selection in the Test Team to play against England for the mythical 'Ashes', and his certain selection as captain of the New South Wales team to meet Queensland on New Year's day.
>
> —*Truth*, Sunday, 26 December 1920

On 28 July 1920, just over a month after they met, Claude visited Dorothy and wrote her a prescription—one of several later removed from Ingelbrae by police—to be prepared at Sinclair's pharmacy at Lindfield. It was for a tonic containing strychnine and belladonna (for poor appetite and digestive problems), digitalis (for heart palpitations), and caffeine as a stimulant. His second surviving letter to Dorothy, dated only some subsequent Friday, reveals they had begun to meet outside professional appointments. He mentions a road map, suggesting a rendezvous somewhere away from Lindfield. 'Yours longingly', he finishes. If this is his first serious flirtation with a woman, he seems adept enough. He goes on to refer to Dorothy's belief in spiritualism and telepathy:

a common interest among her female contemporaries, especially those who had lost loved ones in the War. Specifically, he mentions the writings of Arthur Conan Doyle.

A recent convert to the cause, Conan Doyle had left England in August 1920 for a six-month lecture tour of the New World. By mid-November, travelling with his second wife, three children, secretary and maid, he reached Sydney, where he settled his entourage in Petty's Hotel and was quizzed by a receptive local press on everything from spiritual destiny to England's chances in the cricket. Three well-publicised talks at the Town Hall followed; the last, on the afternoon of 19 November, broke attendance records for a matinee, despite the rival attraction of the touring English team playing their first Test match against New South Wales. In the following days he and his family watched the cricket and met a variety of local personalities, including Norman Lindsay and the war poet Leon Gellert.

At the end of November, after a public reception at the Town Hall attended by some 3500 people, the party moved to the Pacific Hotel at Manly for ten days' surf bathing. Here, Conan Doyle was stung by a bluebottle and went on a picnic lunch organised by local admirers. When he and his party left for England in early February 1921 he had conducted twenty-five meetings in Australia and New Zealand and spoken to some 50,000 people.

Meanwhile, on 16 August 1920, Claude had written to Dorothy again: a brief note that suggested she was to be in Manly in the near future. His next letter, again dated only 'Roseville, Friday', was his last before they began their affair. Here he presented her with a double bind, asking her to pull back from their relationship, to rely on her 'purity and strength', while simultaneously assuring her of the intensity of his desire.

Dorothy was in an impossible situation. Claude had promised passionate, even transcendent, love, while telling her not to tempt him. For the moment at least, he wrote, he was content to 'glide on the river of bliss'—a reference to the Garden of Eden in Milton's 'Paradise Lost', where an amaranthus flower, symbol of immortal love and spiritual faithfulness, blooms beside a stream beneath the Tree of Life. On reflection, this seems a particularly ill-advised letter to write to a lonely woman—even if Claude's 'small conscience' does sit on the bank and 'show the danger signal'.

Sometime soon after this, the affair was consummated—'one day he just forgot everything, and now we are eating our hearts out', Dorothy wrote to her mother—and lasted from late August to late November. At some point, a silver locket with a lock of hair inside changed hands.

In reality, the relationship was probably little more than an affair of the mind, fed by its forbidden nature and snatched encounters, rather than an idyll of unfettered passion. Hanging over them both were the worthy reputations of their families, ready to be brought into disrepute by any scandal. And the liaison was fraught with practical difficulties. Living at Ingelbrae was the ever-attentive Miss Fizelle, while at Shireen Claude's mother Beatrice answered the telephone and kept her son's appointment book. Claude's practice was demanding. His professional stationery (on which he wrote Dorothy's prescriptions), listed weekday surgery hours between nine and twelve in the morning, two and four in the afternoon, and seven to eight in the evenings. On Saturday he was available for three hours in the morning; on Sundays and public holidays by appointment.

Claude also had his cricket career to distract him. Besides playing for the Gordon Cricket Club, he participated in matches at State level, although he excluded himself from some due to his professional obligations. Having missed selection for a New South Wales team scheduled to play the visitors on 19 November, he was chosen instead for an Australian Eleven, captained by Warwick Armstrong, to meet the English in Brisbane on 3 December 1920, in the lead up to the Test proper.

'I don't suppose that at the moment there is a sounder player in the state' — Frank Iredale in the *Sun* newspaper. Claude Tozer sits directly behind Warwick Armstrong (front, centre) in the Australian cricket team, the 'Gabba, Brisbane, 1920. Photo: Davis Sporting Collection: SLNSW call no. PXE 653 Vol.10/201

Claude was now caught up in a double bind. The affair, if it became public knowledge, would have cost him his livelihood and professional reputation. His sporting career might also have come to an end. To be named as co-respondent in Dorothy's divorce would be disastrous. And even if they reached an agreement that Dorothy would leave her husband and children, would it have been wise for him to marry an older woman, in uncertain health, who might never bear him children of his own? Reflections like these may have caused him to make abstract decisions that, on his return to Sydney, he found harder to implement than he expected.

There was the question, too, of his friendship with another young woman, about whom he had not quite yet got round to telling Dorothy, although his mother was aware of it. Was Claude's apparently cold-blooded decision to marry, as a way of solving their impasse, genuine? If he had found a true romantic interest elsewhere, was he trying to soften the blow to Dorothy by protesting his unchanged affection for her? Or was it simply a misguided bluff to help him make the break? At any rate, his departure for Brisbane in late November 1920 coincided with a marked decline in Dorothy's health. Worse still was the threat of his being picked to play cricket for Australia in England the following year, which would involve an absence of many months.

Around this time, according to Miss Fizelle, Dorothy began to talk more frequently of her own death: Harold now was 'never sure whether he would find his wife alive or not', as he told the Coroner.

'Sometime in November' Dorothy 'lay in a fainting fit for a couple of hours', Miss Fizelle testified. A similar event occurred on a Sunday later in the same month, when she accidentally set the bed alight while cleaning her gloves with benzine. Dorothy 'became hysterical', said Miss Fizelle, and imagined that her children were burning—when in fact they were at church in Tryon Road.

Throughout December, her mental state continued to deteriorate. On 2 December she bought laudanum from the pharmacist James Johnstone—taking advantage now of a social connection (the drama society) for a suspicious purchase, rather than resorting to her local chemist. Johnstone warned her that an overdose could be fatal.

A week later on 9 December—the anniversary of her father's suicide—Dorothy appeared 'morbid and strange'. Around now, also, came the morning 'in December' when she was due to do some film work at Arthur Shirley's studio in Rose Bay: as an extra among guests at a garden party, Shirley revealed at the trial.

Arriving very late after the long journey from Lindfield by train, ferry and tram, Dorothy appeared nervous and upset, said the producer, and seemed to be suffering from paranoia and hallucinations, even hearing voices. As well, her speech was rambling and she was unable to concentrate, and he had difficulty in persuading her to go home.

TWENTY-SIX

The Death of a Ladies' Man

Claude visited Dorothy at Ingelbrae again on the morning of Wednesday 15 December 1920, and wrote a prescription for milk of bismuth (a common cure for diarrhoea) for her son Pat. Again they discussed ending their relationship, but he agreed to come back next day 'to say goodbye'. That afternoon, Dorothy, in a brief burst of energy, made another trip to the city. In a pawnshop in Castlereagh Street she sold a brooch—for less than she expected—then walked around the corner to King Street to buy an automatic pistol from Cowles and Dunn. This time her story—that it was for her husband, in India with Ralph Stock—was patently untrue.

'My Darling Mum', she wrote in a letter that was reproduced in the newspapers only in part. In its early, unpublished section, where Dorothy presented a braver and more optimistic face, she thanked her mother at length for her 'dear letter' and for some enclosed correspondence and photographs from her sister Olive, now living in England. 'It is the nicest gift I could have.'

'You've seen what awful gales we've had, and rain, for

exactly a week,' she continued. 'Our house is damp right along the verandah side, water streaming in. But fair again now, and fearful heat, so steamy. A little green frog was on the doorstep this morning.

'Miss Fizelle and I took the children to a lovely "playlet" at Farmers, and let them see the Christmas toys and shops. We also took them to the break up and concert of their own school. Poppy got a history prize. She looked so lovely and I heard people speaking of her near me. How happy-looking she was, and how beautiful …'

Was this the work of a madwoman who less than a week later was intent on killing her lover in cold blood?

Should 'anything happen' to her, Dorothy added on a page marked 'Later' and 'Private', her mother should look after Poppy and Pat. Notably, after writing in detail of home and children, she made no mention of Harold, who was consistently absent from all her recorded thoughts. Dr Tozer had visited that morning, Dorothy went on, and they loved each other more and more. Having 'crossed the Rubicon' there was no going back, and so they had agreed to part—at least as lovers.

Dorothy was later alleged to have said that she had written 'some letters' on the afternoon of 21 December after shooting Claude—but if she did, it was probably the largely-illegible scrawls on the back of her torn-up photograph and Claude's business card that she was referring to.

In any event, having begun her letter to her mother sometime after Claude's visit on Wednesday, she then took to her bed and remained there for five days.

Claude visited as promised on Thursday morning and wrote another prescription for a nerve tonic, again to be made up at Sinclair's, the local chemist. He visited again, for the second last time in his life, on the Friday.

※

On Friday 17 December 1920, at the Cricket Ground on the old military parade circle behind Victoria Barracks, the excitement was palpable as the first Australian Test match after the War began. The Englishmen had arrived in Perth in late October and played a one-day match against the West Australians that ended in a draw. They went on to beat the South Australians in Adelaide and, in mid-November, won again against the Victorians in Melbourne.

In Sydney, in a match against a New South Wales team beginning on 19 November—the one watched by Sir Arthur Conan Doyle—they received their first defeat. Three more matches followed in Brisbane and Toowoomba, of which England won two, against Queensland and Toowoomba sides, and in early December they drew again against an Australian team in which Claude Tozer, as opening batsman, scored two half centuries. By mid-December the English had returned to Sydney, where again they drew a game against the New South Wales Colts on the 15th and 16th.

The following day, eager to see if the Australians could continue to turn the tide, a crowd of some 50,000 gathered in bright sunshine in the SCG stands and on the Hill. Fired up by wartime patriotism and with their mood buoyed by the recent New South

Wales victory, the spectators were only too ready to enjoy their first Test match in eight years. Australia won the toss, and the visiting Englishmen began splendidly, with the Australian side descending ignominiously from 2 for 140 to 267 all out.

On the second day of the Test, Saturday 18 December, Dorothy was still in bed. Having made the break final, as he believed, Claude did not visit again that morning. Dorothy waited in vain for him to relent. At the SCG, the English batsmen were falling swiftly to the Australian bowlers and were dismissed for 190 in their first innings.

On Sunday 19 December, a rest day, both cricketing sides attended picnics at Manly and Newport beaches. On that day, Miss Fizelle would later tell the Coroner, Dorothy appeared dazed and seemed not to see things that were handed to her.

However, sometime on that same Sunday, in a period of lucidity, Dorothy composed another letter, telling Beatrice Tozer that on his last visit (Friday 17), her son had told her of his plan to marry someone else—he was 'not engaged yet, but hoped to be'. Knowing that he could not refuse to come if she, his patient, asked for him, Claude probably hoped that this seemingly brutal act would put a finish to it all. His stated reason—'he had come to the conclusion that it was better for a medical man to be married'—does not suggest that his affections were seriously engaged elsewhere, but now, perhaps, he had sealed his fate. Did Dorothy add some last lines to her letter to her mother, having decided that this was a betrayal too hard to bear?

'May God forgive me. Goodbye my precious Mum.

It is history repeating itself. I cannot help attracting men as this last year has proved, but I never thought or meant to be wicked,' she wrote.

On the third day of the Test, Monday 20 December 1920, Australia batted and took their second innings to 5 for 332. Claude spent the afternoon at the Sydney Cricket Ground, and was spotted by the *Referee* magazine's writer on the Hill, sitting with Percy Kippax, father of 22-year-old Alan Kippax with whom Claude had recently played in Queensland.

On the morning of the fourth day, with Warwick Armstrong batting strongly against England's slow bowlers to reach his century in less than two hours, Claude—summoned by Harold—left his mother's house at Roseville to call on Dorothy.

Obviously considering Dorothy well enough for him to leave her, Harold had already left for work. He would later claim to have no inkling of the cause of her current misery, despite having 'discussed things' with her during just the previous day. Florence also apparently did not find the situation abnormal. She helped Dorothy to tidy her bedroom and attend to her toilette, and Dorothy was composed enough to perform these small tasks.

Sometime after eleven, Claude arrived, obviously disturbed: pale and ill-looking, according to Florence. It had begun to dawn on him that he was caught in a trap of his own making, and that Dorothy would not willingly give him up. There is no evidence he had intended to visit her that day; after a few 'observational calls' he had planned to go to a luncheon at the cricket ground, and then spend the afternoon at the match. That evening, said his mother, he was to take a young lady—his fiancée, according to *Truth*—to the theatre. Beatrice had laid out his fresh linen in preparation.

Apparently entirely rational, Dorothy got out of bed, wearing her nightgown and kimono, and accompanied Claude to the drawing room so that she might give him her small parting gift. He sat on the Chesterfield settee and began to write a prescription. She, with some forethought, had already left the pistol in the room, out of sight on a shelf, or (less likely) concealed in her flimsy nightclothes. It was now about half-past eleven.

On the following day, Wednesday, the fifth day of the test, the flags at the Sydney Cricket Ground flew at half-mast and the Australian players wore black armbands—as they had done once before, mistakenly—as a mark of respect for Claude. The Australian side, with a record 581 in the second innings, clinched the match against the English by an outstanding 377 runs. On the same day, the NSW Cricket Association announced that, in consequence of Dr Tozer's death, Ward Prentice would lead the New South Wales team to meet Queensland at the SCG on New Year's Day. The Australians went on to win the second, third, fourth and fifth tests.

TWENTY-SEVEN

The White Poppy

Page 523: Opium—Probably the greatest of all causes of this enormous increase in the habit within the last few years is its reckless and uncalled for use in medicine. It is the custom of many physicians to prescribe opium in some form for almost every ache and pain which they encounter in practice ... it should be avoided as much as possible, as the opium habit is likely to be contracted. We have met a number of cases in which the habit was acquired in this way ...

—ON THE USE OF OPIUM, LIQUOR,
CHLORAL AND SIMILAR DRUGS

—*Ladies' Guide in Health and Disease*
by J.H. Kellogg, M.D., London

Two items of evidence that emerged at the Coroner's Court in March 1921 were either overlooked, ignored or deemed inadmissible at Dorothy's trial a few weeks later. These were, firstly, Harold Mort's testimony that his wife's previous physician, Dr Bell, had 'had to give Mrs Mort drugs for fear that she would break down again'; and secondly, Florence Fizelle's observation that 'medicine was delivered to the house' after Dr Tozer's visits. Both statements were reported in the *Sun* on the afternoon of the inquest, and in *Truth* a week later, but omitted from all the morning papers.

By 1920 drugs such as potassium bromide, chloral hydrate and morphia were commonly used to treat nervous disease and hysteria, along with various herbal and electrical remedies. If Dorothy were not already self-administering any of these, laudanum might have been prescribed by Dr Bell for any of her complaints of neurasthenia, depression or insomnia. Notably, the medicines with which Claude was treating Dorothy were never explored, despite his being said to be writing a prescription at the time of his death.

Many of Dorothy's earlier symptoms—amnesia, confusion, lethargy, paranoia, delusions and hallucinations—could indicate opiate abuse. The lengthy 'fainting fits' in November 1920 suggest an inadvertent overdose: Ralph Stock recorded that on his *Dream Ship* in 1919 he had doctored a sick passenger with a 'generous dose' of laudanum from his medicine chest—to his consternation, he wrote, the man lay unconscious for fifteen hours. After her arrest, Dorothy's behaviour might too have been affected by her withdrawal symptoms, complicated by whatever medication her doctors used to sedate her and help her to sleep.

Later, reported Florence, such occurrences became more common. Her confusion and lack of concentration at Arthur Shirley's film studio in early December is consistent with drug use. Then on Sunday 19 December, two days before Claude's death, Florence further noticed that Dorothy was dazed, talked a lot, and seemed unable to see or grasp objects placed in front of her.

Two and a half weeks before, on 2 December, Dorothy had bought 'six drachms' (21.3 millilitres, or nearly six teaspoons) of laudanum from the pharmacist James Johnstone—normally a lethal amount, as Johnstone himself affirmed. Pharmacist and author Gail Bell calculates that Dorothy's 'six drachms' of laudanum, taken as a single dose, would yield just over 200 milligrams of pure morphine, or roughly ten times the tolerable amount, and a potentially fatal dose for a novice user or person in ill health.

Finally, if Dorothy had indeed swallowed the whole of the bottle's original contents around midday, and not had her stomach washed out until some eight hours later, the morphine would have been absorbed already into the bloodstream. To reverse its effects would require a specific antidote, and none existed in 1920. This, Bell confirms, indicates that Dorothy survived the overdose and subsequent coma because her body was already accustomed to large amounts of the drug—or otherwise she was extremely lucky.

Among the expert witnesses who gave evidence at Dorothy's trial, the Government Medical Officer Dr Arthur Palmer and prison doctor Robert Lee-Brown were both highly experienced in criminal matters, and yet neither appeared to consider the likelihood that Dorothy might be a drug addict. Nor, it seemed, did the investigating police or crown prosecutor, who might both have been expected to look for every possible explanation for Dorothy's condition other than an exculpatory insanity. The newspapers were also surprisingly circumspect, after *Truth*'s initial disclosures. Did none of them want to see what was apparently so blatantly before them?

In Sydney in 1920, morphia addiction, where it existed, was generally associated with Chinese opium dens and prostitutes in the seedier end of town. Among middle-class suburban housewives, habitual drug-taking, like alcoholism, was often well concealed or unrecognised. But then, respectable North Shore matrons accused of violent murder were an even rarer phenomenon.

Opium, from the Papaver somniferum or white poppy, was first cultivated on the shores of the Mediterranean over 30,000 years ago. Called the 'milk of paradise' and 'destroyer of grief', it was the first medicine used to relieve emotional pain.

Harvested in Asia by bleeding sap from the swollen seed pods, the precious substance was pressed into balls and wrapped in oiled paper before being packed in ceramic bowls and cushioned with poppy trash in chests for export. Reaching Europe in the 1500s, this versatile addition to the *materia medica* was administered pure or dissolved in water to deaden pain, induce sleep and calm distress. Alcohol soon proved a better solute: Paracelsus, in Germany, produced a tincture of brandy mixed with crushed pearls, henbane and frog spawn, and called it 'laudanum'. In the 1600s the English physician Thomas Sydenham refined the preparation: two ounces of opium to one of saffron, flavoured with cinnamon and cloves, and steeped in a pint of Canary wine. Laudanum, he wrote, was a gift from God.

Robert Burton, in the *Anatomy of Melancholy*, noted its particular efficacy for insomnia. By the 1800s the writers Samuel Taylor Coleridge, Edgar Allan Poe and Thomas de Quincy had all celebrated its use.

In 1842 a New Yorker by the name of William Blair described the 'gradual creeping thrill' that occupied his body, lulling pain and producing a pleasing glow from head to foot: 'So vividly did I feel my vitality ... that I could not resist the tendency to break out in the strangest vagaries, until my companions thought me deranged ...' The drug was seductive for its vivid, dream-like hallucinations and mild euphoria. One observer likened it to a continuous gentle orgasm.

By the late nineteenth century phials of the drug, now made up of one or two parts in ten of morphine, was commonly stocked in English apothecaries and grocery shops. Patent remedies, with comforting domestic names such as 'Godfrey's Cordial' and 'Mrs Winslow's Soothing Syrup', soothed coughs and quietened colicky babies. But now, also, came warning signals. Those who took it medicinally at first believed they could give it up at will. But inexorably the dosage would increase, in both amount and frequency, until the exhilaration ceased and drowsiness came almost at once, so that for hours on end they would sit half-dazed, unaware of what they were doing.

Women, it seemed, were particularly susceptible. A nineteenth-century study revealed that of 300 customers of New York drug stores, women outnumbered men by nearly three to one. A third of these were prostitutes, but many were middle-class women, 'of neurasthenic disposition', whose doctors had initially prescribed the drug as a medicine. Sooner or later, the effects invariably included poor memory, disordered nutrition and enervation: the last felt most strongly when the user was deprived of it.

In many users, it was observed, the change in their behaviour was so deceptively gradual that initially it went unnoticed by family and friends. But it was when they were forced to give it up that they suffered most: often it was only the compulsion to get more that kept them from self-harm.

TWENTY-EIGHT

Outside the Drawing Room Door

Miss Fizelle, in her uneasy position between paid companion and domestic servant, never revealed what she knew about the lovers. In the days after 21 December 1920, in her interviews with journalists and police, she gave varying accounts of her strange inaction in the hours immediately following Claude's death. It was not until some three months later, with the Coroner's Report, that her explanation emerged that she had apparently lain in a dead faint for a number of them. But by this time she had had ample opportunity to reflect on the example of Dorothy's own 'fainting fits', some of which had lasted several hours. In any event, due to this alleged period of unconsciousness, Florence had no need to explain where she was when, sometime after the first shots, Dorothy, in the drawing room, fired a fourth bullet into her own breast—a shot that neither Florence nor anyone else appeared to have heard.

Coming to at around three in the afternoon, Florence managed to occupy herself for a further four hours, until seven in the evening, while Dorothy at some point slipped back into her bedroom unnoticed. Between distracting the children from whatever might be going on behind the locked doors, bringing her mistress iced water, and begging unsuccessfully to be allowed in, Florence, it appeared, had simply dithered. Nor did she—despite apparently having a second dining room door key in her possession—attempt to enter the drawing room to discover Dr Tozer's fate for herself.

Did the loyal Miss Fizelle, panic-stricken, simply stall for time while she waited in vain for Harold to arrive and take charge? Or, torn between head and heart, duty and common sense, did she find herself unable to betray her mistress's secret?

But no matter what Florence had done, it would have made no difference. Claude Tozer had died instantly of a bullet wound at around 11.30 that morning.

Dorothy claimed that sometime after shooting Claude she swallowed laudanum and then, while lying in his arms, shot herself. Regaining consciousness around 3 p.m., and finding herself still alive, she waited until the house was quiet and then surreptitiously slipped out the dining room door and back into her own room. Having failed with both bullet and narcotic, the impulse to kill herself had passed, and she did not try again, although three bullets remained in the gun. This decision was made irrevocable when she left the loaded weapon in the drawing room near Claude's right hand. By seven that evening she was walking agitatedly up and down in her room, and when interrupted by Florence, she resisted strongly and tried to conceal her wound.

By around 8 p.m., however, she was in a semi-comatose state and, as her condition worsened, Dr Murray washed out her stomach and administered an antidote. According to Mrs Beeton's advice in 1923, this could have involved a weak solution of Condy's Fluid pumped through a rubber siphon, then twenty grains of sulphate of zinc or a tablespoon of mustard in water, followed by tepid water. While all this was happening, police officers searched the bedroom and helped Dr Murray with the stomach tube. What he administered hypodermically is unknown.

Examining Dorothy earlier, Dr Murray had found a wound from a bullet that he thought might have entered near her heart and exited under her shoulder blade—or, as he told journalists next day, vice versa. In the newspaper stories and the trial transcript the terms 'Colt revolver' and 'pistol' were used interchangeably. Mr Cowles the gunsmith, however, identified the firearm as the popular .32 Automatic Pistol—or Colt Model 1903 Pocket Hammerless—designed by John Browning in 1899 and later manufactured by Colt in America. Unlike the larger and more cumbersome Colt revolver, it had no rotating chamber and loaded eight bullets (rather than six) from a magazine slipped into the butt. With the first cartridge in the chamber, the weapon could be carried fully-cocked for a rapid first shot, after which the empty shell was automatically ejected and replaced. Although accurate only at close range, it was also small, light and easily concealable.

Returning on Wednesday morning at seven, Dr Murray found Dorothy only 'slightly comatose'. Calling again in the late afternoon, he thought her 'only a little confused' and physically much improved. However, this was not what he told police and newspapers at the time, which was that Dorothy was in a critical state. With thirteen police officers still roaming the house and searching for evidence, Murray stalwartly refused to allow them to talk to her.

Nevertheless, when on the same day Dorothy asked to see Claude's mother, Beatrice both agreed to come, and was permitted to sit at her bedside alone. Beatrice, with great self-control, sat and listened while Dorothy described her son's death, and then questioned her on various details. Dorothy's voluntary and coherent account—or, as Dorothy herself probably believed, deathbed confession—suggests that she had thought of a suicide pact as a way out, though it is unlikely that Claude would ever have considered it.

Neither, for a moment, did Beatrice, who demanded that Dorothy tell her the truth.

Despite this apparently rational interlude, by midday next day Dr Murray was satisfied that his patient was out of her mind. He allowed the police brief access, and Dorothy refused to make a statement. She was also lucid enough to ask that her letters to Beatrice and her mother not be posted, no longer wanting them read by their intended recipients.

At Royal North Shore Hospital that afternoon, medical staff told journalists that she was rational, unperturbed and progressing favourably. However, a day later she had again regressed, according to the same doctors' testimony at the trial. Afraid she might make another attempt on her life, Dr Erasmus Bligh ordered her to be kept in isolation and constantly watched. He had difficulty making her sleep, he said, and had to dissuade her from confessing to him.

Despite being a witness for the prosecution, Dr Arthur Palmer agreed with Dr Bligh and Dr Buckley that Dorothy was now certifiably insane, and probably had been so for some time. Like the other doctors, Dr Palmer demonstrated a familiarity with the terms of the McNaughton Rule, describing Dorothy as incapable of understanding the nature and quality of her acts. At the inquest Dr Palmer had not been prepared to classify her condition. By time of the trial three weeks later, however, he had committed himself to the same description—'emotional insanity'—used by Dr Bligh for the defence.

'Emotional insanity'—defined as 'insanity produced by a violent excitement of the emotions or passions, although reasoning faculties may remain unimpaired', or otherwise as 'a passion that for a period creates complete derangement of intellect'—had been used as a controversial legal defence in America as early as 1850. Essentially, it was posited that a person could be sane up until the time a crime took place, insane while it was committed, and sane again soon afterwards. Today the law similarly recognises 'non-insane automatism', where a person is for a short time not responsible for their actions, while some psychiatrists might put forward 'disassociation'—a fugue state removed from reality—or 'post traumatic stress disorder' in a similar defence.

Mrs Mort's Madness

Parts of these doctors' testimony—that in the hospital Mrs Mort spoke in a rambling way, did not know where she was, and thought she heard her children's voices—was reported in the press under the emotive banner headlines EVIDENCE OF INSANITY and ACCUSED'S HALLUCINATIONS.

Two days after the events, on Sunday 26 December, Dorothy—seemingly rational once more—allegedly confessed again to Nellie Manktelow, once she had established that Nellie was a policewoman. At this time Sydney's handful of female probationary constables were not issued with uniforms: having been recruited as a wartime measure since 1915, their main function was to act as 'social and moral guardians' to women and children who found themselves in contact with the police. Nellie kept this conversation to herself until sixteen days later, and admitted in court that she had made no notes of it at the time. Nevertheless, she was able to recreate it for the prosecution in remarkable detail. By the time of the trial, Nellie, who had been widowed a few years earlier, had recently remarried—again to a police officer—and had retired from police duties.

Two days later again, on 28 December, Inspector Leary, with a covey of court officials and journalists, visited Dorothy at Royal North Shore Hospital to charge her with murder. If Leary felt at all slighted at her claiming not to recognise him, he might well have remembered that when he had first encountered her lying semi-comatose at Ingelbrae, he was just one of a number of strange men visiting her bedroom at intervals.

On 6 January, two weeks after confiding in Nellie

Manktelow, Dorothy confessed—for a fourth time—to Alfred Marden. As had Nellie Manktelow, Constable Marden maintained that he had cautioned her in advance, and that Dorothy said she did not care. Marden's account varied slightly from Manktelow's: Dorothy said she had hidden the weapon on a ledge rather than in her clothing, but again she described her actions with great exactitude and in almost identical words. The marked similarity of the two accounts makes it seem probable that Marden and Manktelow had compared notes, or otherwise led Dorothy with questions that ensured her statement tallied with the forensic evidence, or both.

At Long Bay, Dorothy initially seemed determined to make the best of things. An unsigned entry in the gaol medical book notes that on her arrival she told the attendant physician—most probably Dr Lee-Brown—that she felt well and was getting stronger. Everyone had been very kind to her, she said, and the car journey there had been 'splendid'. This medico recorded that he observed no mental deterioration, and that she seemed quite rational and coherent. A few days later, he wrote, she engaged him in a long conversation about books, and asked for a work called 'Shadow Show'.

This was a small volume by one Arthur St John Adcock, a prolific but minor English poet who—along with having a strong interest in Sir Arthur Conan Doyle—had edited several editions of patriotic poems about World War I. Published in 1907, *The*

Shadow Show collected Adcock's light verse on cricket, theatre, politics, literature and love, and included—somewhat bizarrely—a comic poem about a cricketer who addresses his lady love as his inspiration while playing.

The doctor brought her the book, and she talked with him at length about spiritualism, remarking that she was 'afraid such subjects were not suitable for many people'.

'Said that she had a lot of troubles, but seemed perfectly coherent,' he noted again.

TWENTY-NINE

In Long Bay Gaol

For in and out, above, about below,
'Tis nothing but a Magic Shadow Show
Played in a Box whose Candle is the Sun
Round which we Phantom figures come and go

—OMAR KHAYYAM: *The Rubaiyat of
Omar Khayyam of Naishapur*, verse 46

In the prison Entrance Book photographs taken a few days after her sentencing, Dorothy Mort looks immeasurably plainer than before. Painfully thin, her mouth is set in a pinched line, her eyes are underlined with dark rings, and her thick dark hair is tied back in a lank and careless knot. Her long oval face looks sallow rather than pale, and her simple white blouse is knotted at its deep vee-shaped collar with a narrow black ribbon.

Mrs Mort's Madness

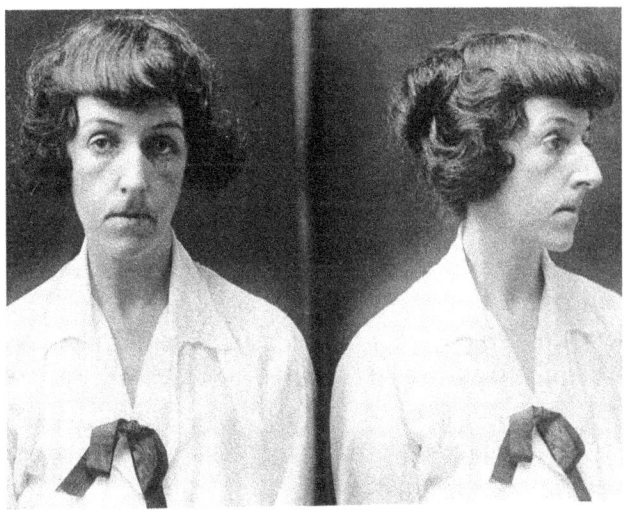

Dorothy Mort on entry to State Reformatory for Women, 18 April 1921.
Photo: State Records of New South Wales, Series Number NRS 3/6007 No 518
Series title: Identification card 1921

Upon arrival at the Entrance and Admission block, her details had been taken down in a ledger, where the printed column heading 'Ship and Date of Arrival' was crossed out and 'Place of Birth' carefully substituted in ink. A yellowing prison file card gave her birth date as 5 November 1885, her conduct and education as 'Good', her religion as Church of England, and her occupation as 'home duties'. She possesed no particular identifying marks. At five feet five inches tall, with brown hair and grey eyes, she weighed 84 pounds. The final notation, 'Detained at the Governor's Pleasure', indicated an uncertain future.

Dorothy's world was now circumscribed by the eighteen-foot sandstone walls enclosing the four acres of ground that made up the new State Reformatory for Women at Long Bay. Beyond the guardroom, the bath and fumigating chambers and the prison clothing store were visitors' rooms where, one Sunday a month, prisoners were permitted a supervised visit of twenty minutes. Past these again was a vacant area where, between the asphalt paths, the sandy soil had been levelled for flowerbeds and grass. Here, women in grey smocks dug vegetable plots and tended the poultry yard that served the prison kitchen. At its centre was a circular shed. When the prison complex had opened to laudatory press coverage a dozen years before, this had been described as 'a roomy pagoda surrounded by palms, staghorns, ferns and potted plants, for the use of lady visitors and others'. It had also housed a cage of canaries. In the exercise yards, divided off from each other by twelve-foot-high iron bars, more prisoners, their eyes cast down and in silence, circled in single file under the watchful eye of wardresses in the central drill room.

The cell blocks or Halls, four massive wings of dark liver brick roofed with corrugated iron, radiated out at right angles to each other. Inside each, sixty or seventy-two single cells ranged along a ground-floor corridor and second-storey steel gallery. A steel net spanned the central well so that inmates might not jump or fall to the concrete below. At the end of each floor was a modern steam-heated semi-circular communal bathroom. Other buildings in the complex housed an administrative office, wardresses' quarters, punishment blocks, laundry and sewing rooms, and two hospital wards.

In line with a new progressive policy, innocent

young girls were shielded from older lags through twelve scientifically-graded classifications, each linked to its own discipline, work and exercise regimes. These ranged through 'Fourteen Days and less' and 'Young and Hopeful Cases' to 'Previously Convicted, Old Offenders', 'Inebriates', and 'First Class Prisoners, two years and over'. 'Diseased' prisoners—those diagnosed with venereal infections—were housed separately.

Within this bureaucratic framework, several hundred women—mostly repeat offenders sentenced for minor crimes ranging from vagrancy, pick pocketing or shoplifting, some for abortion or disposing of unwanted babies—were catalogued. Typically working class and impoverished, often Irish or Aboriginal, these were the domestic servants who stole from workplaces, or the unemployed single girls detained for such mundane offences (frequently euphemisms for prostitution) as being drunk and disorderly, creating a nuisance, or simply having nowhere to go. In early 1921, apart from Dorothy Mort, only three women were in Long Bay for murder. Sentenced to life, or at the Governor's pleasure, they were not in danger of execution—however, rising grimly into the sky over the wall of the men's prison next door, and plainly visible from the women's yards, was the ominous shape of the gallows.

Press interest in the case did not end with Dorothy's sentencing. In the *Bulletin* of 14 April 1921, a week after the trial, an anonymous writer contended that the police had bungled the investigation, and their shortcomings alone had led to Mrs Mort being acquitted.

Their one duty, wrote 'A Lawyer', was to prove that Dorothy 'knew what she was about' when she committed the crime, but instead—by indiscreetly babbling about sensational letters, and passing on 'hideous' crime-scene photographs to the newspapers—they had turned the case into a *crime passionel*. By gratuitously providing 'thrilling evidence' from which insanity could be deduced, they had ensured that the argument for a woman distraught was put from both sides. If the officers had concentrated instead on proving murder, and nothing else, then justice might have been done. As it was, the business left a bad taste in the mouth. Not long before, the writer noted, a woman had been charged with murdering the man who lived off her earnings from the streets, and one who had mistreated her in a way calculated to drive any woman mad:

This wretched creature was not housed luxuriously in a gaol hospital; she was not given an armchair in court; no wardress fanned her assiduously ... The police contented themselves with the plain performance of their job, and the unfortunate from the underworld went to gaol. They did so much more than their job in the Mort case as to suggest that murder is likely to be condoned where the assassin's social position is high, regardless of the public interests involved, which demand not only that guilt shall be punished, but that the proceedings shall be invested—at any rate by the Crown—with as little false pathos, eroticism and melodrama as possible.

Neither was Beatrice Tozer ready to leave the court's verdict unchallenged. On 16 April, under the headline MRS TOZER FOR THE DEFENCE, *Smith's Weekly* entered the fray with a story subtitled: 'The Mort tragedy is finished—The Tozer tragedy remains'.

Smith's Weekly, an irreverent nationalistic rag started two years before by newspapermen Joynton Smith, Claude McKay and R. C. Packer, positioned itself as a crusader for the underdog—and particularly if the underdog were a returned soldier. On the paper's behalf, a journalist called John Drayton conducted a regular 'Court of Public Opinion', whereby anyone who felt himself wronged could 'take it to *Smith's*'. If 'Jack' Drayton believed a case could be made, he splashed it over the front page.

Now Beatrice Tozer was taking Sidney Mack to task in printer's ink for traducing the memory of her only son. To get his client off the hook, Beatrice argued, the Defence lawyer had allowed Dorothy to be branded an adulteress, and Claude a vile seducer and betrayer. Surely, despite his mistakes, his letters to Mrs Mort proved that Claude was chivalrous? Wasn't it solely the word of a woman found to be insane that had condemned him? Now he was longer there to defend himself, must she bear the loss, not only of him, but of his reputation too?

Beatrice was convinced that Claude's fourth letter, declaring his love and referring to their 'platonic existence', was evidence that her son had neither seduced Dorothy nor had sexual relations with her. Her assumption—apparently because it was dated only 'Friday', and referred to their meeting the following 'Tuesday'—was that the letter had been written on

Friday 17 December 1920, in the week preceding his death. Beatrice was almost certainly wrong, however. At this date Claude had already told Dorothy of his plan to marry someone else, and they had agreed to part as lovers, so that this 'platonic' letter was hardly one he would write on the day he came to bid her goodbye.

Neither had Dorothy herself accepted the court's proceedings, according to a series of cryptic notations in the prison Inspection Book. On 23 May 1921, some five weeks after *Smith's Weekly* published Beatrice's complaint, Dorothy applied to the prison authorities from the gaol hospital ward to be allowed to 'make a statement', and this was granted. A few days later she gave a letter to the Comptroller General of Prisons, John Darcy, to be handed to the Minister for Justice. On 7 June she made a similar application, this time for permission to write directly to Beatrice Tozer.

Jack Drayton, in the interim, had evidently realised the fallacy of Beatrice's conjecture, as he made scant mention of her original claim in his next front-page article. Under the headline MRS. MORT CLEARS TOZER'S NAME, which ran across five columns of *Smith's* on 23 July, Drayton—while warmly commending Beatrice's maternal devotion—now limited himself to saying only that, insofar as Claude's written words proved anything, they showed that he was neither a seducer nor a betrayer.

Beatrice Tozer, isolated in her grief and her deep-seated belief in her son's honour, had been convinced that despite any scandal-mongering by the press, Claude would be vindicated when Dorothy stood up at her trial and made the same confession to the world that she had made to Beatrice herself, wrote Jack

Mrs Mort's Madness

Drayton. Instead, Dorothy had remained mute, and Mr Mack had damned Claude in the world's eyes by a selective presentation of the evidence.

A few weeks ago, Drayton continued, Beatrice had received word that Dorothy wished to get in touch with her. At Mrs Mort's request, she had visited her in Long Bay, where Dorothy had told her she wanted to make atonement. On hearing that Mrs Tozer's one desire was to have her son's name cleared, Dorothy had declared that she would make a sworn statement to prove him guiltless.

Beatrice wrote to the Attorney General Edward McTiernan to ask that Dorothy's statement be made on oath and published in the press. The Acting Under-Secretary, Mr Davis Jamieson, replied for the Justice Minister that he could not legally direct that the statement be taken, but that she was free to publicise anything Mrs Mort communicated to her. On 12 July Dorothy wrote to Mrs Tozer on a pre-printed 'State Penitentiary' letter-form.

'Since I have been here I have come to realize many things,' she began. 'One of them is the awful wrong I have done to your son.'

I want to tell you that never at any time did he ever take advantage of me, and that all the things he was accused of were absolutely untrue, and it is a continual horror to me to know that I have left a different impression somehow in the mind of the public. No one could have been more chivalrous than he was. As I have grown stronger I have wished more and more that you should have known this from me, and I am writing this to try and make some atonement for the wrongs that were done to the memory of a fine man.

This was signed, 'Praying for your forgiveness, Dorothy Mort', with 'Brokenheartedly yours' inserted above the signature afterwards. A week later Beatrice wrote to ask Dorothy if she had any objection to the letter being made public, and Dorothy replied briefly: 'No, I have none at all, if it is going to clear your son's name, which would never have been besmirched if my health in that court had been as it is today.'

Both letters were reproduced with Drayton's front-page article of 23 July.

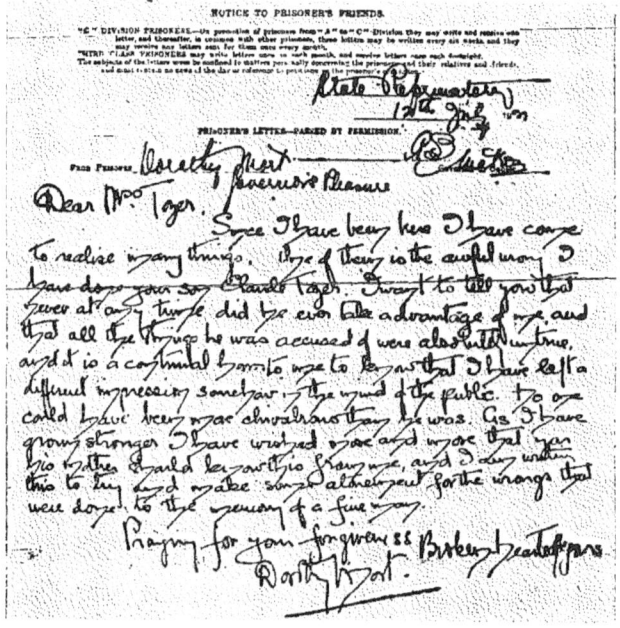

Dorothy Mort's letter of 12 July from Long Bay Gaol asking the forgiveness of Beatrice Tozer for the death of her son. *Smith's Weekly* 23 July 1921

'The long, lone fight of mother love has now closed in victory. Claude John Tozer, who is dead, yet lives again through and in the faith of the woman who bore him', finished *Smith's Weekly* in its usual inimitable style.

❧

In the meantime, on 10 June 1921, Dorothy had been removed from the prison hospital to the Hall where her fellow murderesses were kept in isolation. After being conducted along the steel staircases to the cell rows—resembling, to one observer, 'the bare, cold pigeon holes of a giant filing cabinet'—she was led to a concrete-floored box measuring thirteen feet by seven and a little over ten feet high. This was furnished with a single light bulb, an electric bell, a steel-netted window to the outside, a small marble shelf for her possessions, a mug and a spoon, and some sort of rudimentary sanitary arrangement.

After twenty-two weeks inside, Dorothy's regime began with a bell rung at six. The prisoners were required to be dressed by 6.30 a.m., when breakfast was brought in, and then the cells were locked again until eight, by which time beds must be made. After this, the women went to their assigned tasks in the laundry or needle room. Dinner—soup, a meat dish and vegetables—was served from twelve to one, then sewing or reading was permitted until supper at 4 p.m. Then the cells were padlocked again until six next morning.

As a concession to her health, Dorothy was allowed an iron bedstead in place of the canvas hammocks that the other women customarily rolled and stowed each morning. She was also assigned a special diet, prepared with the other meals in the prison kitchen by a team of inmates in well-laundered smocks and caps, and then carried by each prisoner in a container to her cell at four. Dorothy was also exempted from kitchen, laundry and sewing duties, as well as from exercise and inspection musters.

By 25 August 1921, despite the intervention of a Mrs Reid from the Prisoner's Aid Association, Dorothy was still forbidden access to the prison library. In early September the visiting surgeon recommended she be allowed to make envelopes in the No. 2 needle room, and to exercise in the No. 1 yard, although her attendance was still required at the hospital daily. A month later Dorothy requested to be treated as 'a third class prisoner'—the category assigned after a probationary several months of good behaviour. Privileges gained would include use of the library and attendance at lectures and concerts, more purchases from her work earnings, and being allowed to have her cell light on for longer at night.

Beyond the walls, details of Dorothy's life in prison continued to be scrutinised for political purposes. In August 1922 questions were asked in State Parliament as to whether her unusual visit to the city by tram in mid-February that year, accompanied by a wardress, to see a dentist for urgent attention to her teeth, had been authorised by the Department of Justice.

On 10 January 1924, according to the *Sydney Morning Herald*, Harold Mort approached Mr Kessell, of the Justice Department, about his wife's continuing ill health. Subsequently, Mr Kessell and a Sydney doctor (who turned out to be James Isbister, who had treated her mother and brother) visited her at Long Bay. Dr Isbister found that an operation was necessary: 'not a matter of life and death', but the omission of which would have an effect on her life. Sir John Macpherson, the Professor of Psychiatry at Sydney University, was also called in and concurred that the operation should proceed. Dr Isbister agreed to perform it at his private hospital, and the prison authorities agreed her temporary transfer there.

However, when this information was conveyed to Dorothy, she refused. Unless she was assured that she would not be returned to gaol, she declined to consent to the operation, the *Herald* reported. The matter was to be left in abeyance until Mr Ley, the Minister for Justice, returned from a visit to Melbourne—when, it was thought, the matter might go to cabinet.

Predictably—and after a female member of the public wrote an angry letter to the press complaining about Mrs Mort's preferential treatment—the Minister refused to allow Dorothy her freedom, even for a few weeks prior to the operation to build up her strength. Mrs Mort was to remain under escort the whole time, wrote the *Herald*, and would be returned to prison afterwards. Mr Ley also pointed out that he had no power to compel her to undergo the procedure. The operation was not performed. At some point, due to her continuing ill health, Dorothy was returned from her cell to her original quarters in the prison hospital, where she slept in a private area screened off from the rest of the ward. She was also permitted to wear her own clothes.

In the years that followed, Dorothy became more quiescent. Her next appearance in the Gaol Hospital ledger was on 26 August 1925, when she asked to see an eye specialist. Two years after that, in February 1927, when she was forty-two, the unnamed operation took place during a three-week sojourn at the Coast Hospital. In September 1928, after nearly eight years in prison, she put in a request for a wireless to be placed in the hospital wing. 'Will consider' was the only noted response from the Comptroller. In January 1929—again for undisclosed reasons—she was sent once more to the Coast Hospital.

A prisoner released late in 1928 told *Truth* newspaper that Dorothy was scrupulously neat and tidy in her appearance, kept to herself, and spoke only when spoken to. Viewed by other inmates as delicate and well educated, by this date she had been entrusted with the supervision of the prison library.

How much Dorothy had to do with the other women prisoners in this period is hard to gauge. Due to overcrowding, the system of segregating inmates according to the seriousness of their crimes by now had largely broken down. Another long-serving offender was the transgendered Eugenia Falleni, sentenced by Sir William Cullen in October 1920, who in the persona of Harry Crawford had killed the woman living with him as his wife. According to Dr Herbert Moran, a prominent Sydney surgeon who had followed the case, Falleni engaged in a 'sentimental liaison' with a fellow murderess, but he did not state that this was Dorothy. Nevertheless, the two did become friends. Falleni, who was reputedly illiterate, also served as a trusty in the library, and it was said that Dorothy taught her the rudiments of reading.

Despite her privileges, Dorothy's world was still governed by the clockwork timetable of the prison: a monotonous routine of bells and the regular provision of unappetising food. There was the discomfort of summer heat and winter cold, despite the newfangled heating system. Each day was like the last, broken only by periodic medical inspections, visits from the chaplain, and an occasional audience with the superintendent. On Sunday in the non-denominational chapel, recently completed outside the prison walls by the men's work gangs, the women were seated in a special upstairs gallery designed to keep them from the view of the male prisoners.

Each month Harold Mort visited, driven out to the prison by his younger brother Stanley. While Dorothy endured her long and largely undifferentiated days at Long Bay, Harold, at the other end of the city, lived out his own sentence. Throughout his working life at the Railway Department—by 1925 he was Assistant to the Chief Engineer for Railway Surveys—his Sunday churchgoing, his dinners at the University Club and the polite applause of his fellow members as he delivered his papers at the Engineering Society or the Royal Zoological Society, he stoically endured the gaze of the world.

In 1922, the year after Dorothy was sentenced, Harold had moved from Ingelbrae to 13 Milner Street, a quiet road in Mosman. Helen Woodruff, now in her sixties, kept her promise to Dorothy and moved in with him to look after Poppy and Pat. In a sombre, dark red-brick house behind a heavy screen of trees above Mosman Bay, no doubt they drew some mutual emotional comfort from each other, bound together by the fact of Dorothy's absence. But whatever knowledge Harold possessed of the events of December 1920 he kept entirely from his daughter and son.

The writer Nancy Phelan, a niece of the barrister Sidney Mack, remembered the two Mort children attending Mosman's Killarney kindergarten. There was an air of mystery about them, she felt; they were both pale and quiet and withdrawn, and eight-year-old Poppy—a sweet-faced child with long fair plaits—was very protective of her younger brother. Nancy, then aged about six, believed initially the pair was motherless—but when, feeling sorry for Pat, she asked if he could come to their house to play, she was shocked to hear her grandmother remark in a bitter voice that their mother was in gaol for murder. This pronouncement so alarmed Nancy that she never revealed it to anyone.

By the late 1920s Dorothy still had not faded from public memory, and a disparate group of people had been working towards her freedom. The Act of 1898 had stipulated that, when the Inspector General of Lunacy found no further cause for their detention, persons detained at the Governor's Pleasure could be discharged at the discretion of the Colonial Secretary. This decision was now the province of the New South Wales Cabinet, who took their recommendations to the Governor to be ratified.

Mrs Mort's Madness

In January 1927 the *Sydney Morning Herald* briefly reported that, despite receiving a petition with more than 200 signatures, the Honourable Mr William McKell—Justice Minister in Jack Lang's twenty-month-old Labor Government—had declined to recommend Mrs Mort's release. In November the following year the agitations of Mrs David Stewart Dawson, a well-known socialite, were equally unsuccessful: *Truth* newspaper (a fierce opponent of moral laxity, and always quick to notice it) opined that there were more deserving cases to which she might direct her attention.

In February 1929 the Women's Organising Committee of the Australian Labor Party sent a deputation to John Robert Lee, Minister for Justice in Thomas Bavin's new Coalition Government, to ask for her discharge. Mrs Mort was not now considered a danger to the community, noted the press, but medical opinion differed as to whether her insanity was likely to recur. Mr Lee promised to submit the matter to Cabinet.

In late March David Robert Hall, a barrister and ex-Labor Minister for Justice, wrote to the *Sydney Morning Herald* pointing out that while a judge or magistrate decided whether a criminally insane person was sent to prison, now it was a politician who determined how long he or she remained there. In his time, he continued, this was largely resolved with the help of medical advice. Assuming that Mr Lee adopted the same view, when would Mrs Mort be freed?

Hall listed four prominent physicians—Dr Chisholm Ross, visiting medical officer at the Reception House for the Insane at Darlinghurst; William Siegfried

Dawson, now Professor of Psychiatry at Sydney University; Dr A. W. Campbell, a neurologist; and the surgeon and conservative politician Dr Earle Page—who unanimously favoured her immediate discharge. The late Dr Robert Lee-Brown, 'an alienist of considerable experience', who had seen Mrs Mort daily in prison for seven years, had repeatedly assured him that he had observed nothing abnormal in her conduct. Lee-Brown had also believed she could be safely given her freedom. If Dorothy had been in an asylum rather than a prison, her incarceration would have ended years ago, Hall added. Her friends would doubtless provide assurances as to where she would live, and no one would accuse Mr Lee of taking undue risks in approving her liberation.

The State Cabinet finally relented on 14 October 1929, nearly nine years after Dorothy had entered Long Bay. 'Jack' Lee, elected to the seat of Botany in 1920 and made Minister for Justice in 1927, was later much criticised for the early release of prisoners.

Dorothy was photographed on Wednesday 16 October 1929, the day before she left the prison. Now in her mid-forties, with her hair cut short in a far-from-glamorous bob, her mouth still reveals something of the vulnerability that must have once so appealed to Claude. Her face, remarkably unlined, retains a certain bony hauteur, while a single string of pearls frames the hollows of her throat. For the close-up head and profile pictures, however, she lowers her forehead so that her long fringe completely obscures her eyes.

Mrs Mort's Madness

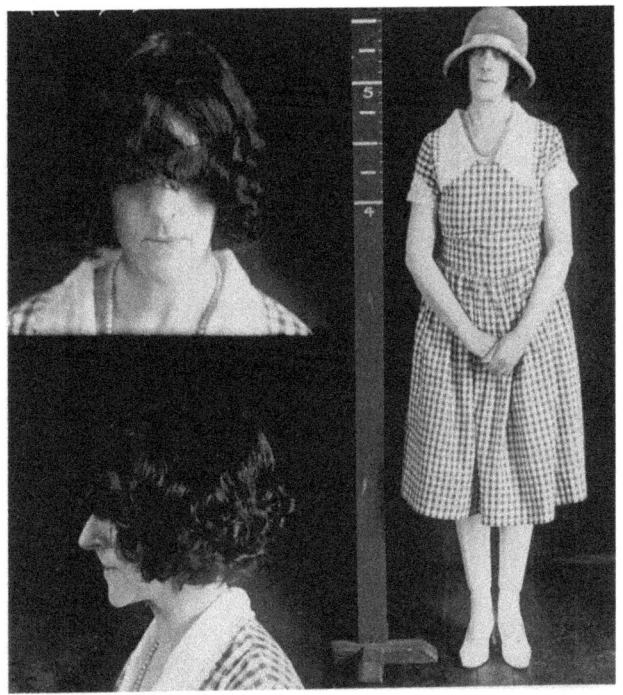

Dorothy Mort, 16 October 1929, on release from prison. Photo: State Records of New South Wales, Series Number NRS 3/6008 No. 773 Series title: Identification card, 1929

The full-length shots reveal that she is wearing a tent-like cotton frock in black and white checks, a fashionable but unflattering garment sent to her by friends before her release. Hanging just below the knee, its dropped waistline and large, square white collar combine to make her look thick and dumpy. On her head is an outsize cloche hat. Only her legs, slender in white stockings and high-heeled shoes with criss-cross straps, point to her former elegance. On her left hand are her wedding and engagement rings. Nevertheless, this cuckoo-like image stands in stark contrast to the procession of nondescript women, old and young and in sadly poorer clothes, whose battered faces surround hers in the Prison Description Book.

Dorothy's release was achieved with almost complete secrecy, according to *Truth*. To prevent tip-offs to the press, even senior gaol officers were kept in ignorance. On instruction from the Justice Minister, the Comptroller-General of Prisons Mr William Hinchy personally delivered the release order to the Prison Governor a little after eight on the evening of 17 October 1929. Harold arrived at 8.30 p.m., the gates were discreetly opened, and Dorothy was helped into the car.

Truth, frustrated at Long Bay, was reduced to staking out the house at Milner Street. When a journalist inquired if Mrs Mort wished to thank the people behind her release, Harold emerged—his 'once-erect and square shouldered body now bent and stooped'—to state courteously, 'We have nothing to say.' When the paper tried again next morning, a tired-looking Harold repeated that they wished to be left alone. The *Truth* photographer had to content himself with photographing the trees concealing the front of the house. Other journalists waited at the docks, hopefully scanning the faces of passengers departing on the *Marama* and the *Maheno*, but reports that Dorothy would be among them quickly proved false.

Mrs Mort's Madness

After her release Harold and Dorothy continued to live at Milner Street, and later at Kirribilli, before retreating to Wamberal and Umina on the New South Wales Central Coast. It was a quiet life, by all accounts. Poppy was seventeen and Pat fourteen at the time Dorothy was set free. Harold moved on up through the hierarchies of the Railways Department and the Royal Zoological Society. Later he donated a great many specimens to the Australian Museum's conchology section.

Dorothy—called by her family 'Dorrie' in later years—was 'a quiet, kind person', Stanley's daughter Margaret told me. The Morts, too, were not unkind. While Dorothy was away, Mrs Woodruff was always included in their family Christmases, along with Eirene's long-time partner Nora Weston. Harold would often arrive at their home to play billiards: it was Stanley, the youngest of the brothers, who supported him most. All through the long years while Dorothy was in prison, Margaret had continued to believe that her father was driving Harold to visit his wife in hospital.

So successful was this veil of silence that Pat's and Poppy's own children did not find out until middle age—and then only through a newspaper story—that their grandmother had once been the subject of a celebrated murder trial.

THIRTY

Harold's Secret

And that seemed to be the end of it.

I had found no further traces of Florence Fizelle after Dorothy's trial in April 1921, but it did not concern me greatly. Florence was a peripheral figure—involved in the events merely by chance, and then only for a few months. A newspaper photograph showed her approaching the courthouse in a pale dress, but with her head bent so low that her wide hat brim entirely shielded her face. After this appearance, she seemed to have slipped invisibly into the interstices of history.

It was only a chance connection that led me to look further. One day I noticed in an art encyclopaedia that the well-known Australian modernist painter, Rah Fizelle, was born in 1891 in Baw Baw, a tiny hamlet in the Goulburn region that seemed no longer to exist. Florence Fizelle, I remembered, was also born in Baw Baw, in 1893. There were only a few Fizelles in the Sydney telephone book and a few phone calls later I was directed to a number in western Sydney. A quiet female voice answered and confirmed she was related to the artist Rah Fizelle. I said that it was his younger sister

Florence that I was most interested in.

'Florence,' said the voice, 'was my mother.'

I was taken aback. Because Florence had disappeared so thoroughly from the public record, I had assumed she had neither married nor had children. I asked, somewhat awkwardly, whom her mother had wed.

'She didn't,' answered the voice calmly.

Some time later in our conversation my informant remarked, 'I may as well tell you. My father was Harold Mort.'

❧

Sometimes, when the light falls in a certain direction, the shadows make objects in a room appear in a certain way. When the light moves, the shadows fall in a different manner again. The facts—the objects in the room—don't change. But suddenly the whole picture looks different.

Ruth was twelve years old when she found out she was Harold Mort's daughter. She had needed a copy of her birth certificate before sitting for a bursary examination. Born in 1933, Harold's last child had arrived some five years after Dorothy's release from prison.

Ruth spent her first six years, until 1939, living with her mother in a rented room in Summer Hill. This was in a large old house converted into flats, as many were at the time. During the War years a lot of families were without fathers, and few people asked questions. Ruth herself didn't ask many, either. As a child, with so much else to inquire about in the outside world, you tend not to question things within your own family, she told me. Whatever you grow up with, you take for granted, and there were few other children in the flats with whom to compare her situation.

'Was your mother a religious woman?' I asked.

Florence had taken her to Sunday school as a child, said Ruth, and went to church with her when she was older. She was not certain if her mother was a Christian, but she believed she was.

After I had hung up the phone, a thousand questions occurred to me. All my prior imaginings were thrown into doubt. The story I had been exploring, and which I had thought belonged safely in the realm of history, to be lightly played with in my self-appointed role of detective researcher, had unexpectedly clubbed me over the head with a present reality.

A week later, I drove out along Parramatta Road to Homebush, in Sydney's west. Ruth's street was a wide, sunny avenue lined with old box brush trees and a mix of Federation houses and new brick apartment blocks. The footpaths were filled with family groups of Indian background; women in salwar kameez pushing strollers, an old lady in a sari with long grey hair crossing at the lights. Following Ruth's directions I climbed several flights of stairs at the rear of her modern block and, behind a screen door, found the neat, quiet flat where she was waiting for me in a comfortable sitting room. On the walls were several of Rah Fizelle's watercolour landscapes of Spain and Italy; the rest of the flat was lined with shelves filled with a great variety of books.

Over tea and biscuits we talked. The photographs

of Florence that Ruth brought out were more flattering studio portraits, showing her mother with a gentle expression and accentuating her large, expressive brown eyes. Again we went back to the beginning: her mother had come to the city on her own when she had left home after the War, but two of her sisters were already there. Geoff was teaching in Bathurst or Blainey, Vere was in the Molong district, but the twins, Heather and Rene, were living in Sydney.

After his return from the Western Front, Reginald—Rah—Fizelle had gone off on a different tack from the others. Gassed, his hearing partially lost, his left forearm crippled after being almost severed by shrapnel, he returned traumatised by what he had seen, disillusioned at the pointless waste of human life, and resentful of his strict Methodist father for his patriotic wartime speeches urging young men to sign up. An iconoclastic loner, Rah—'Fizz', as his friends had called him—gimpy-armed and brusque, had wanted to get away into beauty: 'to look at clouds'. In May 1920, when Florence took up her post as paid companion to Dorothy Mort, Rah was studying at the Julian Ashton Art School and living a Bohemian life in a studio up some steep stairs in Lower George Street. In 1927 he returned to Europe on a travelling scholarship. When he came back, he took up teaching art again.

Florence had also once longed to be creative, and call her life her own, I realised now. In later years she had taken on the sort of jobs where she could work in solitude, and use her hands. But in 1921, a young woman of normal desires and passions, she had found no outlet for them.

Meanwhile, after Dorothy had gone to prison, Harold had sold Ingelbrae and was living quietly behind a solid red-brick façade at Mosman. Helen Woodruff—who was not seen at the trial—had returned from New Zealand and moved in with him sometime afterwards.

Ruth didn't know when or how her mother's relationship with Harold had come about. Sometime after the War—before or after her time at Ingelbrae—Florence had worked in May Moore's photographic studio. In 1922 she became a nanny or housekeeper for a Mr and Mrs Robert Smyth Cranna in Warwilla Avenue in Wahroonga: Mr Smyth Cranna was a draftsman with the Railway and Tramway construction branch. Later again she took a post with the Foleys in Drummoyne, friends of her own family. Perhaps it was from something her mother had said, thought Ruth, but she assumed the affair hadn't happened until after the events of 1920. Florence, she believed, would have fallen in love, and loneliness might have played a part.

By the end of 1932, however, Florence knew that she was going to bear Harold Mort's child. Ruth was almost certain it must have been an accident, and that Florence would have felt the disgrace keenly. Florence chose a location where she was not known to bear her baby. Following a long and difficult labour Ruth was born late at night on 12 May 1933 at Richmond on the Hawkesbury River. Because the doctor was battling hard to save both mother and child, the exact time of the birth was not recorded, so Ruth was never sure if her birthday was held on the correct day.

'My mother was nearly forty,' she told me. 'I don't

imagine she wanted to have a child—and certainly not out of wedlock—but she loved me and protected me. I'm sure she would never have considered adopting me out, nor any other dangerous option.'

Although Ruth believed her mother would have liked to have married Harold, she also thought that Harold had made the right decision in not putting both their families through the further scandal of a divorce—especially as the newspapers would have gleefully raked over the murder trial, now over a decade old.

At 86 Kensington Road in Summer Hill, where mother and daughter had their single room with a kitchenette and a bathroom shared with the other tenants, Ruth happily explored the rambling garden and tried to climb its old Camphor Laurel tree. Her mother now called herself Mrs Ford. Harold provided some furniture, and two pounds a week—enough to get by on in those days—and for several years this sum was their sole support. It was as much as Harold could afford without anyone noticing, Ruth thought. Later they moved to Stanmore, and then to Croydon for three years. Harold continued to visit them once a week.

'He would bring me birthday presents,' said Ruth. 'He gave me books, and once a shoebox full of unusual shells, and a globe of the world. He was quite affectionate, but it was mainly my mother that he talked to. The visits did not seem to be merely a duty for him.'

Her father, she recalled, was fairly tall, clean-shaven

and good-looking for an ageing man, and grey-haired as far back as she could remember. He also had bushy eyebrows, which she had inherited. He did not play games or make up little poems for her, as he had for his nieces and nephews, but she believed that he was a kind man. She had seen a photo of Canon Mort in the vestry of All Saints, Woollahra, and recognised something of him in that.

'We did all have outings together; to an air show at Mascot, or a ride on a steam tram or trolley bus to the beach at Sans Souci, where I remember watching the soldier crabs marching across the wet sand. Once or twice we went to the Museum; more often to the Zoo. When I was about four, I remember he once lifted me up onto his shoulders to watch a procession go past in the city. I don't recall any encounters with anyone who knew him, or who might have recognised him. But if a street photographer tried to take a picture of us, he would always avoid it. I remember him showing my mother a picture in a newspaper once, and pointing out a figure and saying it was Poppy, and I wondered who Poppy was. I always assumed my parents were married, but I never thought to ask why they didn't live together.'

Harold seemed much older than her mother—nearly old enough to be her grandfather. 'When his arthritis became worse we would meet every Wednesday night at Croydon railway station, because he could not walk the distance to our place. He didn't want to go up steps, so he would take the train to a certain platform and we met there, then he could walk back across the platform to return to town. I thought he was called Mr Ford.

'But when I was twelve and we needed my birth

certificate, my mother explained the whole thing to me. The certificate had "Florence Elizabeth Fizelle" as my mother's name, and my name as Ford, and a blank space for the father. My mother told me then that she wasn't his wife.'

Her mother began to call herself Mrs Ford during the last months of her pregnancy, Ruth believed: a short, simple name; chosen because it was common enough to be not easily traceable, and because she had the same initials. 'Before that, I took everything I was told at face value. It never occurred to me that they weren't married, because I thought if you weren't married, you just couldn't *have* children. So I knew then it wasn't right and proper—but it didn't change my attitude much, just my idea of my identity.

'At the same time, I was pleased, because I had read about Thomas Sutcliffe Mort in a history book at school, and so I was quite proud of that. And we had a copy of Eirene Mort's book *The Story of Architecture*—but I couldn't tell school friends that she was my aunt. So that was also something special. Sometimes I've wished that my father had openly acknowledged me, but he chose not to—whether it was to avoid hurting Dorothy, or because he didn't want his children to know, or because he didn't want *anyone* to know.'

If Florence's own parents had disapproved of her situation, it did not alter their kindness to Ruth. As long as she could remember, every second Sunday she and her mother visited her grandparents at their house in Federal Road in West Ryde, to which they had retired in 1928. While Florence cooked the Sunday dinner, Ruth read the Sunday comics or played in the backyard. Agnes had planted a small garden near the rear steps; on the rest of the quarter-acre block her grandfather grew roses, vegetables and a small orchard of fruit trees.

After Agnes's death in 1941, Florence and Ruth moved into the West Ryde house, where Florence looked after Hubert until he died in 1943. Then her mother found a job at a photographic studio, tinting and retouching photographs, and later in a millinery business, decorating hats. By now, Harold was bedridden in a Mosman private hospital, and they would make the long trip by tram and train to see him. Ruth didn't always enjoy these visits: her parents spoke about people she didn't know, and sometimes she found it tedious. In his last years Harold couldn't manage to shave, and grew a beard—never a substantial one—but even now, if she kissed a bearded man, it made her remember her father. Occasionally one of his brothers turned up at the hospital while they were there. Once Dorothy herself visited, but Florence hurried Ruth away.

'My mother was quiet and unassuming, and kept to herself,' said Ruth. 'She would come with me to St Andrew's cathedral in the city rather than go to the local parish church, because she thought in a big church people were less likely to try to make friends with her. I don't think many people could get close to her, and it would have been partly because of all this. Or so I assume.'

When Harold Mort died on 18 May 1950, Ruth, now seventeen, remembered her mother coming into her room early one morning to tell her of his death, having read about it in the newspaper. There was no question of their going to the funeral, but both—in their separate ways—grieved for him.

In 1952 the house at West Ryde was sold and Florence took a position as a paid companion to two elderly ladies at Chatswood. By now Ruth had begun a career as a journalist, starting as a copy girl at two pounds five shillings a week. Around 1961, when one of the old ladies died and the other went to live with her brother, Florence and Ruth moved in together at a new flat at Shirley Road in Wollstonecraft.

'We were very close to each other all our lives, but my mother was very private. And I didn't ask her a lot of the questions that I would have liked to have had answered because I was protective of her, just as she was protective of me.

'I don't think Dorothy knew about any of it. I think that was why we left so hurriedly when she came to the hospital—to avoid any awkward questions—but I thought then that that was what any occasional visitor might do, when the wife arrived to see her husband. I don't know how he explained to her why he was late home on the evenings when he visited us. But I don't think he would have told her.'

Harold left no will—odd, I had once thought, in such a methodical man—and to the end of his life neither acknowledged nor repudiated Ruth's existence. Florence Elizabeth Ford (née Fizelle) died on 17 January 1969, aged seventy-five, in the Home of Peace, Greenwich. Until her final illness she and Ruth had continued to live together at Wollstonecraft.

'My mother did say to me once: don't keep a diary, don't write anything down,' Ruth said. 'It can get you into trouble.'

Ruth had one memento of Harold. When she was

a child, he had given her a copy of Charles Henry Hanson's *Stories of Old Rome: the Wanderings of Aeneas and the Founding of Rome*, published in 1884 by T. Nelson and Sons, which he had won as a prize at The King's School. Inside was pasted one of Eirene Mort's bookplates, designed for him in 1905, bearing the proud motto 'Fidèle à la Mort'.

Waverley Cemetery, early autumn. A stiff breeze blows off the pristine ocean whitecaps and the sun shines brightly in a perfect blue sky. A toy-like red container ship slides slowly across the horizon. Here and there, a towering white marble angel hovers above acres of tombstones and urns, between which run cracked bitumen paths in a complex jigsaw. A stone horse trough is thoughtfully placed just outside the sandstone gatehouse so that long ago the plumed black horses drawing funeral hearses might not go thirsty on just such a warm day as today. Most of the area is Church of England; Italian names dominate on ornate family vaults in a smaller Catholic section, along with a scattering of Hanlons, Duggans and O'Riordans. The poets Henry Lawson, Dorothea Mackellar and Henry Kendall, and the cricketer Victor Trumper, have long lain here in peace, and—since two days before Christmas of 1921—so has Claude Tozer.

Today the place is deserted, the Sunday afternoon silence broken only by occasional birdsong. Among the more austere Protestant markers in weathered sandstone and dull granite is the white marble tablet of Claude's father Jonathan Tozer, who died in April

1917. 'Until the day break' is the text Beatrice chose for him.

Claude is buried next to his father, beneath a matching tablet, and in the spot where Beatrice herself had no doubt expected to lie. 'Thy will be done' are the stoical words that she—still able, evidently, to hold fast to her faith in the face of God's random cruelty—selected for her son. When Beatrice joined them twenty-four years later she was commemorated by the single word, 'Peace'.

Claude Tozer's gravestone at Waverley Cemetery. Photo: author, private collection

I have come unprepared. It has rained recently, the first proper rain after a long dry summer, and bright green grass has sprung up inside the plain sandstone border enclosing the three graves, hiding the few wilting white petunias and oleander blossoms I have been able to gather from among those growing wild near the gatehouse.

Further down towards the cliff face, where the rock shelf is washed by the Pacific, boats on trailers are drawn up casually alongside the cemetery fence, and a pair of suntanned girls in swimsuits and sarongs take a shortcut along the coastal path to reach the cafés of Bronte beach. Climbing back up along the bitumen rise towards the main gate, I am overtaken by a spindly-legged and leathery-faced old man whose brown kelpie follows obediently and—against all the rules—unleashed at his heels. He gives me a tiny smile as he passes, in mutual recognition of another perfect Sydney day.

A Coda

The writer **Ralph Stock** was not in Sydney in March 1921 to explain in court why Dorothy had mentioned his name while buying a pistol at Cowles and Dunn—if indeed he knew. He had left again for Europe on the *Orvieto* in late August 1920. *The Cruise of the Dream Ship*, his most successful book, was published in December 1921, while *The Love Flower* screened at the Paramount theatre in Sydney in September 1922. Stock subsequently made a career as a playwright and screenwriter in England and America. He was still looking for another *Dream Ship*, he wrote, but somehow the renewed quest never materialised.

By early March 1921, when Dorothy was committed for trial, **Arthur Shirley** was reported to be shooting the final scenes of *The Throwback*, but the film was never completed. By September that year his production company was in voluntary liquidation, and the actor-producer was caught up in a series of court battles with his lead actress and cameraman. Shirley was forced to move from the Australia Hotel to a rooming house in Cathedral Street in Woolloomooloo, from where he planned his next project, a successful adaptation of

Fergus Hume's novel *The Mystery of a Hansom Cab*, released in 1925. However, Shirley was never to regain the heights of his former success. 'Towards the end of his life,' wrote an observer, 'still clad in old time spats, a long tweed coat and homburg hat, he drifted from stage door to stage door in Sydney, telling tales of early Hollywood to anyone who would listen.'

The legal practice of **Sidney Mack** continued apace after his defence of Dorothy Mort in 1921, but some colleagues believed that his increasing eccentricity, and habit of making strident political speeches in public places, stymied his chances of being appointed to the Bench. He died at Drummoyne hospital on 25 April 1934, a few weeks after successfully defending Annie Elizabeth Richards, of Narrabri, against a murder charge. Richards was accused of fatally throwing a rock at a man who had tormented her.

'Would you kill a sitting bird?' Mack famously demanded in his final address to a jury.

Arthur Leary retired after thirty-one years of service in January 1933, having reached the rank of Metropolitan Superintendent of Police. In the same year he was awarded the King's Police Medal for an especially distinguished record.

Dorothy's mother **Helen Woodruff** died on 7 November 1943. At the time of her death she was still living at 13 Milner Street, Mosman, with her son Ronald.

After Claude's death, his mother **Beatrice Tozer**

stayed with her brother Leo Charlton at the Rectory in Killara for a time, and afterwards went to live in Manly. In July 1935, when she supplied details of Claude's military career for the University of Sydney's 'Book of Remembrance', she was living at Double Bay, just down the hill from All Saints Church in Woollahra. She died on 24 May 1944, aged seventy-nine.

Harold's sister **Eirene Mort**, after a successful career as an artist and illustrator, went on to teach art at Frensham school in Mittagong. This was run by a pair of redoubtable tweed and tie-wearing Englishwomen with small dogs at their ankles who believed that cold water, fresh air, cricket and Anglican hymns sung beautifully would turn out desirable specimens of Australian womanhood. After her long-time companion Nora Weston's death, and her own retirement around 1960, she spent her final years assembling a series of hand-made books in meticulous architectural handwriting. One of these, *A Bundle of Sticks*, a transcription of hundreds of pages of Mort family letters, suggests that a later generation of Morts believed they were short-changed in the financial dealings leading to the demise of Mort and Co as a family company.

Eirene never wavered in her support for Harold. The engraved bookplates she designed for him in 1905 and 1914 show variations of the same crest, emblazoned 'Fidèle à la Mort'. In 1928, while Dorothy was in prison, Eirene produced a further bookplate for Harold showing a surveyor's theodolite on a broken tripod made of gum twigs knotted together with string and weighted with an empty wine bottle. While it is tempting to read some complicated metaphor here: a broken life repaired by a retreat to the bush, that probably is not the domain of bookplates. Her last design for Harold, in 1934—the year after the birth of Ruth—shows an octopus and seagulls in a rocky seascape. In one corner a chiton—that most tenacious of molluscs—is curled around a book. Another she designed for Poppy Mort in 1921 (the year her mother was taken away from her), shows a naked, winged sea-sprite riding a flying fish, the whole encircled by a garland of poppies.

After Harold died in his Mosman private hospital on 18 May 1950, at seventy-one, **Dorothy Mort** lived with Poppy—now also widowed—at Wentworth Falls in the Blue Mountains. This was no easy relationship, according to a younger relative, although apart from dementia in her old age Dorothy experienced no further episodes of mental illness. Before she died in 1966, aged eighty-one, she ordained that her ashes should be scattered on her mother's grave in the Northern Suburbs Cemetery, and not on her husband's.

Around 1912, according to Lands Department records, the house **Ingelbrae**—first named 'Ingelba', after an Aboriginal place, before its transmutation to more comforting notions of chimney nook and Scottish creek—was built on Lot 11 of the Bonny View Estate, one block up from where Howard and Owen Streets intersected in a dog-leg corner. In 1921 the northernmost sections of these two streets, including

No. 11 Howard Street, were incorporated into Tryon Road.

Sources and Acknowledgements

The events and personalities sketched in Part One of this book, while corresponding in all major aspects to historical fact, are partially fictionalised. The legal proceedings in Part Two are also imaginatively reconstructed: the proceedings were reported in great detail by the press of the day, but the police report to the coroner and the coroner's inquest documents do not survive, and the records of Dorothy's trial (NSW State Records, Central Criminal Court Transcripts, 1921 ref. no. 6/1130 and Supreme Court Depositions ref. no. 9/7255 file 15/21) are incomplete. The sequences of evidence paraphrased in various newspapers contain unacknowledged gaps and were generally presented in an erratic order. In the official transcript of testimony—where it exists—the witnesses' responses to questions have been transformed into a seamless statement. From all these sources I have combined and edited the available material according to my best judgement.

For recollections about the history of the Mort family, and for grace in the face of my persistent curiosity, I am grateful to various Mort relatives who prefer to remain unnamed, to David Mort, and particularly to Ruth

Ford. I have also drawn on the following published sources: E.K. Crace, *The Wreck of the Duncan Dunbar: Ten days on a Coral Reef*, G.S. Heaton and Co, Bowker's Row, UK (no date); Alan Barnard, *Visions and Profits: Studies in the Business Career of Thomas Sutcliffe Mort*, Melbourne University Press 1961; Eirene Mort, *Old Canberra, A Sketchbook of the 1920s*, National Library of Australia 1987; and Penelope A. Starr, 'Wielding the Waratah: Eirene Mort. A Study of an Artist/Craftswoman's Training and Working Experiences from the Period 1879 to 1910', submitted as a BA Hons thesis at the University of Sydney, 1980.

For records of Claude Tozer's medical career in Egypt and France, I am indebted to the Australian War Memorial, Canberra and the National Archives of Australia. In addition to the works of C.E.W. Bean and various editions of the *Sydney University Medical Journal*; sources include L.M. Newton, *The Story of the Twelfth: A Record of the 12th Battalion AIF during the Great War of 1914–1918*, J. Walch and Sons, Hobart 1925; Sue Austin and Ron Austin, *The Body Snatchers: The History of the 3rd Australian Field Ambulance 1914–1918*, Slouch Hat Publications, McCrae, Australia 1995; A.G. Butler, *The Australian Army Medical Services in the War of 1914–1918, Vol II*, Australian War Memorial, Canberra 1940; and Stuart Braga, *Anzac Doctor: The Life of Sir Neville Howse*, Hale & Iremonger 2000. For additional information on military matters I am indebted to Brendan O'Keefe; to Greg Growden, author of *Gold, Mud and Guts*, ABC Books 2001, based on the journals of Field Ambulance member Tom 'Rusty' Richards; and to Leonard May's unpublished diary held in the War Memorial. For their efforts to extend my knowledge of cricket I am grateful to Tony McCarron, Bob Howard and James Rodger. Terry Dawson at Mick Smith's Gunshop on George Street in Sydney was helpful with ballistics, and I was assisted also by John Partridge, formerly of the Department of Corrective Services.

For information about the early days of the Australian film industry I owe much to film historians Graham Shirley and Jeanette Delamoir. The account of the production of *The Throwback* draws on John Tulloch's *Legends on the Screen*, Currency/AFI, Sydney 1981, and film footage from ScreenSound Australia. Copies of Ralph Stock's books, now out of print, are held in the State Library of New South Wales and the British Library—his time in Australia is described in *Confessions of a Tenderfoot* (1913), *The Chequered Cruise* (1916), and *The Voyage of the Dream Ship* (1921). His sister Mabel Stock—whom Ralph calls 'Peter' in *The Voyage*—published her own account, *The Log of a Woman Wanderer*, in 1923. Sir Arthur Conan Doyle's visit to Sydney in 1920 is described in *The Wanderings of a Spiritualist*, Hodder and Stoughton, London 1921.

Medical quotations are from J.H. Kellogg, M.D., *Ladies' Guide in Health and Disease*, London, International Tract Society, 59 Paternoster Row, various editions, first printed 1895. Information on the history of opium comes from Barbara Hodgson's *Opium: Portrait of a Heavenly Demon* (1999), and the Schaffer Library of Drug Policy, USA.

I am grateful to Gail Bell, author of *The Poison Principle*, Picador 2001, and to Stefania Siedlecki and Gigi Santow for an enjoyable correspondence on matters pharmaceutical. Malcolm Ramage and Greg

Woods kindly advised on legal procedures. Others who assisted my research include Paul Bentley, Bruce and Barbara Best, Max Bonnell, David Charlton, Beryl Chesterton, Russell Cook, the late Margaret Coombs, Stan Dellar, Peter Doyle, Mark Ferson, Tracey Fiertl, Pamela and Phillip Fizelle, Bryce Fraser, Bridget Griffen-Foley, Barry Goodman, Tom Havas, Fiona Hibberd, Jill Levenberg, John May, William Mills, Olivia Nelson, Jan O'Reilly, Robert Pauling and the late Nancy Phelan.

I am indebted as always to the State Library of NSW and the Mitchell Library; the National Library of Australia; the Archives and Rare Books section of the Fisher Library at the University of Sydney; the NSW State Archives; the Art Gallery of NSW Reference Library; the Australian Medical Association (NSW) Limited; the Shore School and The King's School archives; the Manly Library and Local History Centre; Ku-ring-gai Library and Historical Society, and the Woollahra Library and Local History Centre. In London, I acknowledge the assistance of the British Library, Imperial War Museum, and Public Records Office. Any factual mistakes are entirely my own.

Finally I would like to thank Wendy Cosford, Kate Grenville, Carl Harrison-Ford, Jacqueline Kent, Jenny Paynter and Marsha Rowe for their useful comments, Gideon Haigh for his encouragement, and my agent Barbara Mobbs, as always, for her patience. I am grateful to Rod Morrison, Jon MacDonald and the Xoum team for the care put into the book's production.

www.ingramcontent.com/pod-product-compliance
Lightning Source LLC
Chambersburg PA
CBHW031422150426
43191CB00006B/365